PRAISE FOR
HERETICS & WAF

"This book is not just for those who identify as women, it is for any one who is tired of hiding in the shadows, living small, or letting others control their lives. If you are ready for a total spiritual shift that will have you loving yourself, believing in your dreams, and living life on your terms, Phoenix is at your side sharing her radical role models, gentle guidance, and exercises for self-empowerment. Read this book, and you'll be inspired, motivated, and activated in all the best ways."

—Madame Pamita, author of *The Book of Candle Magic*

"*Witches, Heretics & Warrior Women* challenges us to rise up and reclaim our powers. With advanced magic and unique methods to experience the three aspects, Phoenix LeFae encourages strik-ing insights, a rewilding of the soul, and the cultivation of true inner strength. This deeply inspired book reminds us we only have one precious life, and it should be lived in our wild, sacred truths. From one rebel to another, I thank her."

—Astrea Taylor, author of *Intuitive Witchcraft*

"This book is for the magical rebels who live in the margins: the change makers, the wise ones, the boundary breakers. *Witches, Heretics & Warrior Women* guides, inspires, and ignites an inner fierce magic while allowing space for imagination and spiritual autonomy. The world is begging for webs of oppression to be torn apart, and this book is rich with tools and allies to get us there.

—Dani Burlison, author of *All of Me:*
Love, Anger and the Female Body

"This book examines the rise and downfall of rule-breakers from Jeanne D'Arc to Boudicca and connects us to the energy of each so that we can learn from their successes and failures alike. *Witches, Heretics & Warrior Women* is a delightful read that opens the doors to possibilities far beyond Maiden, Mother, and Crone."

—Diana Rajchel, author of *Urban Magick*

"A dynamic blend of history, mythology, and magical practice applied to the fine art of pathbuilding. Phoenix has brilliantly paired inspiring figures from world history and mythology with hands-on exercises, workings, and tools to aid the reader in walking the witch's path with confidence and deeper understanding. This book is a wonderful guide for finding personal power while awakening the rebel within. New and advanced practitioners alike will find material that will illuminate their practice."

—Laura Tempest Zakroff, author of *Anatomy of a Witch*

"Once again Pheonix LeFae's unique and beautiful view of the world around her has brought forth great wisdom. Never would I have ever thought to find Marie Laveau, Mary Magdalene, and Boudicca all in the same book, yet here they all are, power houses of femininity, teaching us that it's OK to be rebellious, nonconformist, and absolutely magical; showing us how we can own our witchdom and encouraging us to stick a finger up to the mundane. *Witches, Heretics & Warrior Women* is empowering, insightful, honest, and it encourages us to be the same.

—Tara Sanchez, author of *Urban Faery Magick*

Witches, Heretics & Warrior Women

ABOUT THE AUTHOR

Phoenix LeFae (Sebastopol, CA) is a professional reader, root-worker, teacher, and ritualist. She has been practicing Witchcraft for twenty-five years, and her teachings are connected to the Reclaiming tradition, Druidry, and Gardnerian Wicca. She is also the co-owner of an esoteric goddess shop called Milk & Honey.

WITCHES, HERETICS & WARRIOR WOMEN

Llewellyn Publications
Woodbury, Minnesota

Ignite Your Rebel Spirit through Magick & Ritual

FIRST EDITION
First Printing, 2022

Cover design by Kevin R. Brown

Llewellyn Publications is a registered trademark of Llewellyn Worldwide Ltd.

Library of Congress Cataloging-in-Publication Data
Names: LeFae, Phoenix, author.
Title: Witches, heretics & warrior women : ignite your rebel spirit through magick & ritual / by Phoenix LeFae.
Other titles: Witches, heretics and warrior women
Description: First edition. | Woodbury, MN: Llewellyn Publications, 2022. | Includes bibliographical references. | Summary: "Transformative stories of powerful women from legend and history that will inspire and support you as you connect with your inner rebel" —Provided by publisher.
Identifiers: LCCN 2021043605 (print) | LCCN 2021043606 (ebook) | ISBN 9780738767932 | ISBN 9780738768144 (ebook)
Subjects: LCSH: Witches. | Wicca. | Heretics. | Dissenters. | Witchcraft. | Magic.
Classification: LCC BF1571.5.W66 L47 2022 (print) | LCC BF1571.5.W66 (ebook) | DDC 133.4/3—dc23
LC record available at https://lccn.loc.gov/2021043605
LC ebook record available at https://lccn.loc.gov/2021043606

Llewellyn Worldwide Ltd. does not participate in, endorse, or have any authority or responsibility concerning private business transactions between our authors and the public.
All mail addressed to the author is forwarded but the publisher cannot, unless specifically instructed by the author, give out an address or phone number.
Any internet references contained in this work are current at publication time, but the publisher cannot guarantee that a specific location will continue to be maintained. Please refer to the publisher's website for links to authors' websites and other sources.

Llewellyn Publications
A Division of Llewellyn Worldwide Ltd.
2143 Wooddale Drive
Woodbury, MN 55125-2989
www.llewellyn.com

Printed in the United States of America

Other Books by Phoenix LeFae

Cash Box Conjure

Hoodoo Shrines and Altars

Life Ritualized

Walking in Beauty

What Is Remembered Lives

*To Copper Persephone and Lizann Basham—
what is remembered lives.*

CONTENTS

Disclaimer   xi
Introduction   1

PART I: BEING THE REBEL
Chapter 1: Join the Rebellion   7
Chapter 2: Using This Book   15
Chapter 3: Knowing Thyself   29

PART II: BEING THE WITCH
Chapter 4: The Witches   47
Chapter 5: Circe   55
Chapter 6: Anne Boleyn   73
Chapter 7: Marie Laveau   91

PART III: BEING THE HERETIC
Chapter 8: The Heretics   113
Chapter 9: Mary Magdalene   119
Chapter 10: Jeanne D'Arc   137
Chapter 11: Salome   155

PART IV: BEING THE WARRIOR
Chapter 12: The Warrior Women   173
Chapter 13: Boudicca   181
Chapter 14: Moving Robe Woman   195
Chapter 15: Harriet Tubman   213

Conclusion 231
Acknowledgments 233
Recommended Reading 235
Bibliography 239

Disclaimer

There are lots of suggestions in this book for exercises and exploring that will have you looking at some of your personal baggage. Although I encourage you to do self-exploration, this book is not to be used as a replacement for therapy, medical care, or medication. No ritual, spell, or magickal working should replace professional medical care or advice.

There are also formulas and recipes for herbs and essential oils included in this book. Don't use any ingredients that you are allergic to. If you are uncertain about your reaction to any ingredients, don't use them. Better not to risk it.

If there is anything in this book that you are unsure about, don't do it.

Introduction

Rebels change the world.

Do you call yourself a witch? Do you want to call yourself a witch? If you answered yes to either of those questions, then congratulations! You are a rebel.

Why is that important?

A rebel is someone that rises up against the establishment. Rebellion is the act of pushing back against culturally established customs. Rebels and heretics look at the status quo and think, *Nah, I don't want anything to do with that.* They want to do things their own way and buck restrictions, forced trends, or cultural norms. Rebels are willing to give a big middle finger to conforming.

Witches have been heretics for as long as there have been heretics—hell, for as long as there have been witches. Witches and heretics are totally rebels. They all go hand in hand.

Think of a world where no one questions the status quo. How would that society look? What if we all just accepted things? No matter how bad, broken, or abusive, what if we all just followed along? And let's be real; a lot of folks are happy to live this way. A lot of our society and culture are stoked about the status quo.

Especially if you benefit from the status quo, and quite a bit of our population does, in fact, benefit from the status quo. Many, *many* people are willing to put their heads in the sand and go along to get along.

But not a rebel…

Rebels show us there is another way. They shake up the mainstream and point out the problematic. Rebels are game changers. They walk on the edges, the fringes, and break apart tyranny and abuse. Anyone who has ever stood up and said "No, I won't let this go on any longer" is a rebel.

The world needs rebels. Are you ready to be one?

Witches, heretics, warriors, and truly any human that has refused to "stay in their lane," do as they were told, or just conform are all fighting the battle of making changes in their own way. Pushing back against conformity may only change one thing, one moment, or one life, but the more we push back, the more change happens. Like ripples on a pool after tossing in a pebble. Rebels are willing to lob a boulder into the waters and watch as the ripples spread, a smile on their face and sweat on their brow. Crush the patriarchy!

Although rebels have no gender, I am going to focus on women for a moment. Women have been indoctrinated into being good. We are taught to do as we are told. We are encouraged not to rock the boat. When women speak up about abusive behavior, we must fight to be heard and believed. And we have to deal with questions like "Was it really *that* bad, though?" Too often, women allow themselves to deal with bad behavior, abuse, and oppression because it's easier or more acceptable.

The oppression only gets more intense when we start to factor in things like race, ethnicity, or country of origin. That's not to say things haven't changed and improved over the last several decades. Indeed, they have, but culturally, many of us are still swimming upstream.

This is why the world needs rebels.

There are theories that once upon a time, the world was matriarchal. We don't have solid anthropological evidence of these theories being factual, but even now, there are a few small tribes across the globe that function in a matriarchal way. Modern history is filled with stories of witches, heretics, and warrior women fighting against patriarchal structures. Is this a harkening back to a time before patriarchy was the norm? Is this a calling, a longing, for something different than the society we are a part of?

I don't think that matriarchy is the answer to all the world's problems. I *am* curious what the world might look like if our cultural structure was matriarchal, but I actually believe true balance comes from something else altogether. Something we don't really have access to at the moment. Something that isn't binary. The world isn't that simple, and our societal structures shouldn't be either.

Matriarchy may be mainstream in the future, or it may be something that never was nor never will be, but we can't deny we currently live in a society and culture that is patriarchal. We are all indoctrinated into it and influenced by it in ways we might not even see or fully understand. That's just the reality of modern life. In order for there to be change—in self and in culture—we will continue to need witches, heretics, and warrior women. We need badass people to step up, act up, and show us there is another way.

Are you ready? Do you want to take back your power and unleash it on the world? Pick up your sword, jump on your horse, and let's go! We've got a world to change, babe! One rebel at a time.

Part One

Being the

Rebel

Chapter 1
Join the Rebellion

This book is going to push you out of your comfort zone. It is going to ask you to do some deep reflection. Reading this book is going to encourage you to incite a rebellion in your own life. This is not simple or easy work. This chapter will cover some things you need to know as you step into the world of witches, heretics, and warriors.

Throughout this book I am using the terms *witch*, *heretic*, and *warrior* as synonyms. They are all rebels. The goal of this book is to help you ignite your inner rebel. There are three pathways to rebellion: that of the witch, that of the heretic, and that of the warrior. These terms are the same and yet, each one of them has their own special and unique flavor. There are many ways to step into the life of a spiritual rebel. You get to decide the path you take—maybe you even take more than one.

Is This Witchcraft, Though?

Before we get deeper into this topic and I jump up on my soapbox to encourage you to join me in this fight, I need to answer a bigger question that is going to come up. I can already hear people saying, "What does this have to do with witchcraft?" Well, my dear, it has everything to do with witchcraft.

The harsh truth and reality of witchcraft is that it is more than wearing a certain aesthetic, posting cool images on social media of your altar, and performing spells. An important part of witchcraft—maybe *the* most important part of witchcraft—is taking care of your inner temple.

Carved above the entryway to the temple at Delphi were the words "Know thyself." In ancient Greece this was one of the most important spiritual tenets, and it remains one of the most important spiritual tenets in modern times. This includes on the path of witchcraft. In order to be a successful and consistent practitioner of witchcraft, you have to know yourself. If you want your spells to work, if you want to see real change in your life, if you want things to get better, you must know yourself.

What makes you tick? What triggers the heck out of you? Why? What are your strengths and weaknesses? What are the edges of your personal comfort zone? Do you know and understand your core motivations? Do you know your core wounds? Are you able to work with them as allies rather than letting them control you? The more you are aware of your inner landscape, the more effective you will be in your work, spells, magick, and life in general.

In this book I am going to share spells, rituals, and magick, but I'm also going to ask you to do some housekeeping of your inner temple. I'm going to ask you to become more and more aware of your focus, your desires, and what drives you and why.

It can be hard work, but it is totally worth it. Plus, the world needs you to do the work.

Why Me? Why Now?

The time of playing nice is over. You were born during this time for a reason. Staying small won't work. There is only one of you. There will only ever be one of you. That's pretty spectacular if you think about it. Your job is to be the best you that you can be. I mean, who else is going to do it? The more of us who stand up, step up, and shine, the better the world will be.

Shining brightly and being the best you possible is a rebellious act. Our culture is happy to stay in alignment with the status quo. The status quo is safe. It's comfortable. It's the devil we know. Even if the status quo doesn't work, even if you are totally unhappy, following the status quo is easy because it is the life you already have. To change is to step into a life of uncertainty, and that's scary.

Why do so many people stay in abusive relationships? Why do so many people stay in jobs that suck away their souls? Why do people allow so much unhappiness in their lives? Because it is the devil they know. These are complicated issues. There is not one magick pill that will solve all your issues and there's nothing wrong with being stuck, but there is a better life, and you can have it.

Do you know someone who fights against anything that might shift our culture toward more inclusivity, more social care, and heck, even more humanity? I know I do. Maybe you are the person resisting these shifts. Shifting our culture feels like a risk because the devil we know tells us it is safe right where we are. Why change what we know, even when it's bad, terrible, broken, and not actually working for us? The devil we know, he's a convincing bastard. Change is uncomfortable and even a bit scary, which is why change is an act of rebellion.

Society also believes the fallacy that if something you have is also available to someone else, then you won't have it anymore. People accept a reality of lack and limitation. The truth is, we live in a world of abundance. There is more than enough for all of us. Inviting others to the table doesn't take anything away from you—it brings in more richness, wealth, love, and delight!

If each person nursed their rebel soul and called forth the wild nature within, the revolution would just happen. A new existence would slide into place, its powerful heart beating rapidly, calling all heretics to remove the chains that keep us yoked to the machines of mediocrity.

Imagine if each shining being on earth polished their inner glow and let themselves be seen for the fabulous creature they truly are! The night sky would be lit up from the power of it all. You were not born to be small. You were born to be you, a radical shining star.

BRAVERY

This book is really about bravery. It takes a good amount of bravery to embrace the rebel's way of life. And what I have found is that most folks don't fully grasp the meaning of bravery. You may think of bravery as doing the scary thing, putting your life in danger, or running into a burning building to save the family inside. Yes, these are examples of bravery, but so much bravery is found in the simple moments of everyday life.

Bravery is courageous behavior. Courage is the ability to do something that frightens you. So is it brave to face a fear? Yes, but let's talk about fear for a moment. Fear is the response to facing something dangerous and painful. There are lots of situations in the world that we are (and should be) fearful of, but some of these moments are more insidious than others.

And for some of you, what I am about to say may sound heretical…

SCARCITY

One of the major issues of modern American culture is a disconnection from the wild world and each other. People live in a false reality that says we are alone, have to go at it by ourselves, and must pull ourselves up by our own bootstraps. The wild world is ignored and nature is not taken care of. All this leads to a scarcity issue, and it is one of the symptoms of the patriarchy and capitalism.

The structures of capitalism and the patriarchy tell us that every crumb must be fought for and that there isn't enough to go around. Scarcity tells us there is only so much of something. This might be true with resources like coal and oil, but it isn't true when it comes to love, support, success, and power. These resources are unlimited and endless.

Scarcity pits "us" against "them." It doesn't even matter who the "us" and the "them" are; there are millions of ways we can polarize ourselves against other people. With a scarcity mindset, there are only so many possibilities of achievement. It creates the toxic belief "If I want something, I have to make sure that they don't get it first."

This idea also tells us we'd better act right and stay in line, otherwise we might lose the modicum of support/success/love/ whatever we have and find ourselves suddenly becoming one of "them." Scarcity makes it dangerous to step out and be the weirdo. Because being the weirdo makes you incredibly vulnerable.

VULNERABILITY

We are all afraid of vulnerability. Maybe we aren't all afraid of it to the same extent or in the same way, but it is a normal human reaction to being seen. And yet, the funny thing is, we all desire to be seen. What a paradox!

Have you ever witnessed someone else be vulnerable? Have you ever witnessed someone share something deeply personal, emotional, and hard? Have you seen someone speak in public about something profoundly painful while standing tall and brave? No doubt you have. And how did that make you feel?

Often, when we witness someone else's vulnerability, we remark on how brave they are. It feels so powerful to witness someone else be so open and brave. Occasionally this may also lead us to be vulnerable in return—not always, but occasionally. Bravery can be contagious.

However, internally, raw vulnerability can feel like weakness. How would you feel about being the one standing up sharing something profoundly painful and expressing difficult emotions for others to see?

We don't want to appear weak. We don't want to be vulnerable. We don't want to be seen. We don't want to be judged.

So how can vulnerability be a weakness in ourselves, but an act of bravery in others? This is a truth that rebels understand: Vulnerability is brave, which is why it feels so freakin' scary.

There is a famous quote that asks, "What would you attempt if you knew you could not fail?" I've always loved this quote. It is a quote of bravery. These words ask you to leap and to trust that the net is going to catch you. It is a call to action. Do the thing. Change the world. Try!

I recently read a book by Brené Brown. In her book, Brown levels up the famous quote by asking, "What's worth doing, even if you fail?"[1] This is a quote of bravery in the face of vulnerability.

---

1. Brown, *Daring Greatly*.

These are rebellious words. What would you do anyway, failure assured? This question brings the heat and really asks you to dig deep into your heart and soul.

Both questions are ones of vulnerability and bravery, but from opposite sides of the coin. And these are the questions rebels must ask themselves over and over again.

Failure is not a bad thing. It is not something you need to be punished for or pay penance on. Failure is divinely human. There is no greater teacher than failure, and yet, it is scary because it forces us to be vulnerable.

Humans are such conflicted and complicated creatures.

AUTHENTICITY

Being a rebel requires full and complete authenticity. Being authentic means being genuine. Being genuine means you are who you say you are. All of this boils down to personal integrity.

Two of my high school teachers were powerful rebels, although I doubt either of them would have used that word as a personal descriptor. They both taught at an alternative high school for "dropout" kids, me being one of them. Through my experiences at this school, I learned to find my voice and I discovered a love of learning I had previously thought didn't exist. Another thing I learned through their teaching was the awareness of personal integrity. And in the almost thirty years since then, I've come to discover that integrity is one of the most important tools of the rebel.

Integrity is simply having strong moral principles. However, morality is so ambiguous. What is right or wrong to one person might not be for another. My teachers had a brilliant way to explain personal integrity as simply as possible. It goes like this: "If you're gonna talk the talk, you gotta walk the walk." Basically, say what you're going to do and then do it. Be authentic. Be genuine.

Rebels are deeply immersed in the mysteries of personal integrity and authenticity. Why? Because when you look around at the world and realize things are wrong, even when everyone else is telling you it's okay, you have to listen to your internal voice, the inner compass. At the end of the day, your integrity is the only thing you truly have.

If you say you're going to do something, you need to do it and/or deal with the consequences of not following through. This also means you need to know who you are. Remember what I said about the words above the temple of Delphi? To do this work, you have to know thyself. How can you expect yourself to be authentic if you don't even know what you want, what you like, where you desire to be in life, or who you are?

The truth is that you change, you grow, and you learn. Throughout those changes, the act of being authentic is always constant. It is knowing and listening to who you are right now in this moment and having an understanding of that person and their needs. Being authentic also means acknowledging the fact that it all might change. What you desire now might look very different tomorrow, next month, or in five years.

When you know thyself, you have a better chance of embracing your integrity. This puts you in a prime position to do the work of changing the world. This is what makes you a witch, a heretic, and a warrior.

CHAPTER 2
USING THIS BOOK

Luckily, we have many examples of rebellious and badass women who can help you—and inspire you—to find your own way along the path. There have always been rebels. There have always been witches, heretics, and warriors who were trailblazing, standing up for what's right, and leading others to find their true voice. These women come to us from ancient history, myth, and legend.

In the following chapters you will be introduced to nine women, all witches, heretics, and warriors. Each woman was selected to help you unlock your own heretical heart bit by bit until that power can fly as free as a bird.

Each chapter will offer you a snapshot of the woman's story and include prompts and exercises for personal exploration. These exercises are designed to help you connect with your own rebel heart using the woman's energy as inspiration. Go through these exercises at your own pace, one at a time, or flip through the pages, do a little bibliomancy, and let the exercise you open to inspire you to do the heretical work. There are no rules!

Each chapter will also feature a ritual designed to help you connect to the wise one written about. This is deeply spiritual work. Approach these rituals with the reverence you would approach a saint, Goddess, or revered leader.

This book is for everyone: all genders, gender expressions, personality types, ethnicities, and religious backgrounds. Throughout the book I will use female pronouns and descriptions more often than not. This is not in an intention to exclude, but it is an intentional focus on the feminine, which has been suppressed for thousands of years.

CHEEKY

I'm using the word cheeky here as the Brits do. Cheeky as in irreverent, but in an amusing way. My way of teaching and talking about magick can sometimes come across as cheeky. This is not to everyone's taste, and I get that.

Know that as you move forward in this book, you may be exposed to some of my cheekiness. I take witchcraft, magick, and ancestor veneration extremely seriously, but I am a firm believer in large doses of mirth with my reverence.

It's important that we not take ourselves too seriously, otherwise we might start believing that we hold all the answers and that there is one pure truth. This way of thinking only leads to problems.

RITUALS

There are lots of rituals in this book. Feel free to adjust them as needed to fit your personal circumstances. You are always welcome to substitute ingredients or ritual items that you feel might be more appropriate for you.

Candles

In many of the rituals there is a suggestion to use glass-encased candles of varying colors. My personal preference is glass-encased candles because they are less messy and problematic than other types of candles. However, you can use any type of candle that you have.

It's unlikely that you will burn through an entire glass-encased candle during any of these rituals. You can use the same candle for many, most, or all the rituals, if you feel so called. The candles called for are not consecrated for any one use, and so it is completely acceptable to use them for multiple purposes.

If you do burn through a glass-encased candle, simply recycle the glass or save it to refill and use again.

Cleansing

Before performing any ritual, it is a good idea to do a thorough cleansing. I'm a big fan of cleansing and feel it is one of the most important spiritual practices you can do on a regular basis. There are lots of ways to cleanse. Try these out and see which one(s) you prefer.

- Smoke Cleanse: Burn your favorite cleansing herbs and use the smoke as a purification. Simply move your herbs and firesafe container around your body, allowing the smoke to clear out any negative residual energy.
- Asperging: Dip your favorite cleansing herbs in salted water and sprinkle this over your head and body. You can also use the herbs to gently slap the surface of your skin and clear away anything that doesn't serve the ritual.
- Rattle: Use a rattle around the edges of your body. This will help clear negative and/or stuck energy.

- Salt: Use a salt scrub on your skin or take a bath in salted water. Salt is a neutralizer and will help clear away unwanted energy.

Clean Up

After all of the rituals you will need to clean up your ritual space. Simply put items where they belong in your home. If there is leftover incense or other ritual bits, these can be burned and the ashes can then be spread outside. If there are images that you collected and no longer want, either donate these or burn them and scatter the ashes.

✦ ✦ ✦ Magick ✦ ✦ ✦

You may have noticed I'm spelling the word *magic* with a *k*. When I first started practicing witchcraft in the early 1990s, I was taught that the word *magic* referred to sleight of hand stagecraft, while *magick* is what witches do.

I've heard modern witches argue it both ways and for some, this way of spelling has fallen out of fashion. For me, magick—with the *k*—is what witches do. Therefore, that's how I spell it. Plus, I've got a bit of flair for the dramatic.

Your mileage may vary, and we can still be friends if we disagree.

What Is Remembered Lives

In my book *What Is Remembered Lives*, I talk about this heretical concept of ancestors, deities, and spirits needing *us* to remember *them*. What if they are stronger, bolder, and more accessible if we remember them, tell their stories, and have relationships with them? Because of that idea, it feels like my personal responsibility to continue to tell stories of Goddesses, witches, warriors, and heretics, just so they can live on and continue to do their good works.

In the book I ponder what might happen when the last follower of a specific Goddess dies. What happens when your descendants forget you? There is almost a second death that can happen to each of us.

And now I ask the opposite question: What happens if (or when) our stories are told for hundreds of years after our bodies are gone? What happens when our stories inspire greatness in others? What happens when our history and lives bring inspiration, courage, power, and change for people in the future that we will never know?

It's a heretical act. It's changing the future. How cool is that?

Ancestors

If you were to boil this book down to its truest essence, it would be a book of ancestor veneration. You may think—or have heard—that working with ancestors means learning about your own bloodline or family history. And yeah, sure, that is part of it. But there is so much more to ancestor work.

There are some historical figures who are so bold, wonderful, or terrible that they become ancestors to us all. There are historical names that live in infamy and as a collective, we take them on as cultural ancestors. Yes, this also means collectively, we have some terrible ancestors. Some of whom we are taught about in school as if they deserve to be remembered and honored.

However, there are so many cultural ancestors who are amazing and powerful and deserve our remembrance. These are the kinds of ancestors featured in this book. They may not be of your blood, lineage, or ancestral culture, but they have taken on a level of fame that makes them accessible to all of us.

If you feel a special connection with one of these ancestors, I highly recommend developing your own relationship with that ancestor. Talk to them, leave offerings for them, make space for them in your home and in your heart, and tell their stories to others who may have never heard of them before. It doesn't have to be complicated.

I will be sharing some cultural, contextual, and historical information on each of the women featured in this book, but know that in my research, I read entire books about these people. There is so much more to know than what I have been able to provide. Consider my words a jumping-off point. Go forth and learn more.

✦ ✦ ✦ Working with Ancestors ✦ ✦ ✦

There are many ways to deepen a relationship with an ancestor if you feel a connection.

Reading

Read more about the powerful women featured in this book. There is a lot of information out there about each of them. Do your own research into these titans of our past.

Altars & Offerings

Create a space in your home where you can connect and commune with these ancestors. You can find out about the culture of their time and what objects, decorations, foods, or drinks might appeal to them. Use these items to create a space where you can feel their energy in your own home and communicate with them. Give offerings of foods, drinks, or incenses that they might have enjoyed during their lives. If there are specific charities you feel they would have supported, donate to those causes in their name.

Tell Others

Although the women in this book are famous, they are not names and histories everyone knows. Do something to change that. Share what you learn, teach others about them, and talk about their histories and power. What is remembered lives.

Travel

If possible, travel to the places where these women lived their lives. Go to their shrines and holy places. Visit the lands where they would have walked.

Meditation, Trance, and Journey

A meditation, trance, and out-of-body journey are not all the same thing. However, in many modern witchcraft and spiritual circles, these terms are often used interchangeably. It is important to know the difference and understand the type of working you may be undertaking. There is some amount of overlap in these three processes, and one can easily lead into another. Each of these states takes practice.

For the purposes of this book, there are plenty of places where meditation may be suggested. There will be trances offered. These are opportunities for you to make this work deeply spiritual.

Meditation

A meditation could also be referred to as a contemplation. It is an exercise, or practice, in stillness. In a meditation you may focus on your breathing, on music or chanting, or on a spiritual concept. Most people meditate all the time and don't even realize they are doing it. If you've ever "zoned out" or went on autopilot, you were likely in a meditative state.

With a meditative practice, you want to go from an unconscious zoning out to an intentional focus. Meditation is really easy for some folks, but I've found many of us (like me) who are used to distraction in the forms of social media, computers, and television find it a bit harder to intentionally meditate. Don't let the challenge of it stop you. There are lots of ways to engage in meditation.

Ultimately, what you are trying to do is shift your awareness. The goal is to move from a "talking self" conscious state to a "god self" subconscious state. Repetition is one way to make this shift a bit easier, as your consciousness often needs to be distracted in order for the subconscious to get any spiritual work done.

> ### ✦ ✦ ✦ Meditation Can Look Like ✦ ✦ ✦
>
> • Reciting a mantra
> • Singing a chant
> • Focusing on your breath
> • Watching the wild world
> • Listening to chanting or drumming
> • Dancing, especially in repetitive motion
> • Playing music

Trance

Trance is the next level after meditation. Some liken trance to hypnosis. It's deeper and moves things on a subconscious level. A trance can be self-guided or led by another person. Many folks find it easier to flow energetically from a meditation to a trance to the next (and deepest) level, journey, but that isn't always the case.

With trance, you will find messages and information coming through that you may not have any conscious awareness of. Do these messages come from your own subconscious or through outside entities? You will have to determine that answer for yourself. (My answer to this question is yes.) Often folks who practice trance find they have experiences they would have had a hard time "scripting" or planning out on a conscious level. The story doesn't go where you might expect it to. What happens can sometimes feel like it is happening in a dream state.

Each of the rituals you will find in the following pages contain trances. If you are doing this work on your own, consider recording the trances ahead of time and playing them back during the ritual. If you are doing this work with a group, pick someone ahead of time to lead the trance process. Regardless of the method you choose, the trances should be read slowly, leaving space between sentences. The trance leader must remember to breathe while reading and leave plenty of space for the experience to unfold. Some people meditate or trance very easily, while others need more time. It is best to go slow in order to make space for those folks that need more time going through the process.

There is a myth about trance that everyone has an experience that resembles watching a movie or having a dream. Not all trances are seen like a movie. Although specific imagery may be noted, let yourself engage all your senses. Notice what you feel, hear, and smell. Don't feel like you are doing something wrong if the trance doesn't come to you like a movie. There are lots of ways to have a trance experience.

In this book's trances, there will be points where it says (Pause). This means to keep silent for at least thirty seconds. When the notes say (Long pause), keep silent for at least one minute and up to five minutes. It may feel like a really long time, but trust me, leave the space. You might also consider drumming or rattling during the trance to help you shift your awareness.

Journey

A journey is the deepest of these three states. A journey is the process of your spirit body leaving your physical body and moving through the world or spiritual realms. You may have heard this referred to as *astral travel*. On the astral realm, you can visit anywhere on the planet. You can create your own temples and meet other people who are also out-of-body on the astral plane.

This is not easy to accomplish. Astral travel takes practice, and I have found it easier to move from meditation to trance to journey with the help of a practitioner guiding me through the levels. You will not find journeys in this book.

SUSPEND DISBELIEF

I'm a skeptic, and I think it's a much-needed trait for anyone stepping onto the path of the rebel. However, for the purposes of becoming a rebel and working with the power of witchcraft, I want to encourage you to suspend your disbelief.

That doesn't mean you should stop questioning things. I am not an authority on your life. However, I do want to encourage you to try things that feel weird, silly, or impossible. Witchcraft will ask you to believe things that are odd and outside the norm. A rebel does this easily, but a rebel does not take on any belief that is outside their personal values. A rebel will always trust their gut and personal integrity.

As we move forward, trust your instincts, listen to your gut, and believe the impossible, and you'll start living a rebellious way of life.

TOOLS FOR THIS WORK

There are some tools that will be helpful as you work your way through this book. They can help add to your process, keep you on track, and bring some awareness to the heretic you are becoming. In each section of this book, specific tools are offered. We will dive more deeply into the magick and mystery of each of these tools. Starting with …

The Journal

Now is the time to start a journal for this work or to mark out clearly in a current journal that this work is beginning. Tracking what you are working on and how it is going will give you valuable information about your journey.

As you move through this book, there will be lots of opportunities for self-reflection. Use your journal as a magickal tool to help you track your thoughts and feelings. A journal is a tool of accountability. If the goal is to know thyself, a journal offers you a metric for checking in and checking up on yourself.

In some traditions of witchcraft, the journal is referred to as a *book of shadows*. I've always felt like a book of shadows is akin to an esoteric scientific journal. With a book of shadows, you track your spellworking, moon phases, timing, ingredients, and energy around your spells.

A journal works the same way. It gives you the means for tracking what is going on, what is important, and can often show you the patterns in your life and psyche that you might otherwise miss.

The Witch's Eye

We all have inherent psychic abilities. The use of our psychic skill is like a muscle. Some of us have naturally strong intuitive and psychic muscles and some of us will need to work on building that muscle.

Your witch's eye is another way of describing your third eye, or that spot just above and between your normal seeing eyes. This is an energy center in your body and connects you to your intuitive and psychic self.

Doing the work of the rebel, you will need to work on flexing your witch's eye muscles. Developing your intuition is one way to connect to this energy center. But occasionally, just having awareness of this place on your body can start to open you up to more psychic and intuitive skills.

In the trances included in this book, there will be instructions to open your witch's eye. This means your third eye. Think about this spot like a dial on a stove. You can turn the dial up, opening your witch's eye more and allowing you to "see" more. You can also turn this dial down, closing your witch's eye more and shutting down your psychic awareness.

Practice opening and closing your witch's eye. This may come easily, or you may need to play with this and practice. Notice how this muscle gets stronger the more you use it.

LET'S GO!

You are the one and the time is now.

Take a breath, put your hand on your chest, and feel the beating of your rebellious heart. Go take a look outside. See the beauty of the world. Are you ready to reengage with this world as a witch, a heretic, and a warrior? Take a moment to think about your descendants; those of blood, those of love, those of lineage. What world do you want to leave for the future?

Let's change the world, rebel! Let's change the world.

Chapter 3
Knowing Thyself

Becoming a rebel will ask you to take some uncomfortable steps and even some leaps of faith. The magick of this work is going to challenge you and shake thing up a bit. This rebellion is one of finding the strength and power in yourself. Because of that there are some things that may come up for you, some buzzwords to be aware of, and some questions you might need or want to ask.

TRIGGERS AND GLIMMERS

No doubt you've heard the term *trigger*. It's a helpful psychological phrase that's become sadly overused. Psychologically speaking, when someone experiences a trigger, it can cause severe, painful, or traumatic psychological responses. However, many folks throw the word *trigger* around as a way to describe something that makes them feel uncomfortable or something that bothers or frustrates them. Not quite the same thing.

Discomfort and psychological trauma are not the same. But since this word has taken on a life of its own, I feel it's important to talk about it in the context of being a rebel.

Claiming the title of witch, heretic, or warrior is a potentially triggering action, both on a psychological level and on a level of personal discomfort.

Discomfort is good, even if it doesn't feel good. It's a positive thing. It shows us where our edges and boundaries are. When we bump up against discomfort or frustration, there is a treasure trove of personal information waiting to be explored. Some edges and boundaries need to be pushed and expanded and some of them don't, but only through self-exploration (and knowing thyself) will you be able to know the difference.

The discomfort part of triggers can be like a snake shedding its old skin. It's itchy, weird, and maybe even a little bit gross. We can't rush the shedding process without potentially hurting ourselves. And so, we have to be in the discomfort of it. We must undulate, roll, shift, and move, slowly and with intention. We have to grow through it with patience and care.

This is what it is to be a witch, to be a heretic!

As you put on the mantle of rebel, you will need to start discerning what is a real trigger that may require deeper psychological help and what is actually a personal discomfort, worth pushing against. The work of this book should not replace medication, therapy, or help from professional and trained healers. If you notice your triggers causing pain, flashbacks to abuse, or serious psychological trauma, seek professional help. Therapy is amazing. Help is available.

A trigger can actually be pointing to underlying issues, including feeling:

- Excluded
- Powerless
- Scolded
- Forgotten
- Unloved
- Judged
- Blamed
- Disrespected
- Ignored
- Controlled
- Manipulated
- Trapped
- Disconnected
- Frustrated
- Treated unfairly

As with all things, there is also another side to triggers. Have you heard of *glimmers*? Glimmers are the opposite of triggers, and they are just as important to acknowledge. A glimmer is the thing that lights you up, brings you joy, expands your heart, makes you smile, and brings a sense of awe and wonder to the world.

A glimmer doesn't have to be something revolutionary. One of my glimmers is mac and cheese. I love the stuff. It never fails to lift me up, make me feel better, and lighten my heart. I can eat a lot of it. Another one of my glimmers is a specific memory of a personal sacred site near where I live. I experienced a beautiful ritual in that spot. When I return to that moment in my mind, it never fails to help me glow and remind me of the magick and beauty in the world.

The reason that glimmers are so important is because they are the antidote to triggers. A glimmer has the ability to pull us back from the clutches of a trigger. Having glimmers close at hand is a good way to practice grounding, centering, and clearing energy. The word *glimmer* may sound light and fluffy, but it's deep and profound magick.

I highly encourage anyone stepping into their fullness of being a witch or their rebellious persona to have a strong tool-box of glimmers handy. We must remember to connect to beauty every single day. We have to remember joy and creation.

Being a witch, a heretic, and a warrior doesn't mean you forsake joy, fun, love, and frivolity. It does mean you stand up for what's right, what's just, and what's true, which is really hard work. Sometimes you can get lost in the hidden shadows of that work. Glimmers help us remember why we do the work and find joy in the things that keep us going, make us love, and offer us solace.

A glimmer can show up as feeling:

- Starlike
- Powerful

- Elevated
- Remembered
- Loved
- Accepted
- Included
- Respected
- Free
- Fair
- Connected
- Brave
- Shiny
- Bold
- Smart

Being a heretic and changing the world means you need to own and rock your glimmers. There is only one you in all the world. You owe it to yourself—and to the world—to be the best, most amazing, shiniest, most fabulous you possible.

That's not to imply you have to be perfect or create some impossible ideal of yourself. You just need to be you. Own who you are—all the best parts and the challenging parts. Understand why you react to things the way you do. Receive compliments; like, don't just hear them, but actually take them in. Accept your personal badassery and rock your rebel heart out!

✦ ✦ ✦ Star Stuff ✦ ✦ ✦

Have you heard that people are made of star dust? This is a popular thought amongst many of the witches I know. It's a beautiful, poetic thought. And it's scientifically true as well.[2]

Scientists are pretty much in agreement that the universe started with a "big bang." What was banged is up for debate, but much of what we know of the universe was formed from this explosion. Stars formed, elements were created, and the vastness of space was filled with stuff. Most of the elements that our bodies are made of were created when stars—like our sun—exploded, sending their makeup into the universe.

There are also trace amounts of elements in our bodies that were created during the big bang. That's pretty magickal.

The reason I bring this up is because it is an important thing to remember. Life is hard. We struggle, we grieve, we experience hardship, we doubt ourselves, we worry. Humans are fascinating creatures. *And* we are made of stardust. We are miracles. There is so much beauty in the world, and we are a part of that.

For me, that fuels my rebel soul. Knowing I'm made of stardust makes me want to fight for the other star beings in the world. The building blocks of life remind me we are all important and we need to take care of each other. I am a heretic because of that.

---

2. Lotzof, "Are We Really Made of Stardust?"

AM I DOING THIS RIGHT?

As a metaphysical shop owner and someone who teaches classes about witchcraft, I meet a lot of new seekers to the path. I can tell you the most common question I get is "Am I doing this right?" This question comes in many forms and encompasses virtually anything related to magick: How do I set up an altar? How do I do a candle spell? How do I speak to the Fae? How do I…?

These questions are really about one thing: doing it right versus doing it wrong. Nobody wants to be accused of doing something wrong; that makes us vulnerable. Doing something wrong opens us up to ridicule and shame and could even lead to being kicked out of the cool kids club.

And I get it, friends, I really do. I'm one of those classic perfectionist procrastinators. In my younger days I wanted to be a drummer so bad! I loved the ritual drummers who came to the public rituals I attended, and I was desperate to drum too. My friends even pitched in and bought me a small drum, but I wouldn't play it because I didn't know how and I didn't want to do it wrong.

Here's the secret I know about drumming, twenty years later: There isn't a way to do it wrong. There are certain rhythms and beats that are good to know. There are styles and lingo that are helpful to understand. Certain drums are better for certain types of playing, but there isn't a wrong way to drum.

I wasted close to a decade not playing the drums. I was too scared. I didn't want to fail, didn't want to look foolish. No doubt you can easily find something in your own life where you put yourself through the same wringer.

The thing is, if you never start, you never learn.

Walking a spiritual path (especially the path of the witch, heretic, or warrior) means that you are going to risk trying new things and some of them will not work. That's okay! If you are treated poorly or negatively, if someone with more experience is mean or cruel as you are learning, they aren't worth your time.

No one else can tell you if you are worthy. You simply are. But the fear of being unworthy can keep us frozen and blocked in a self-imposed prison. Anyone willing to step into the path of mystery and magick is worthy of it. Anyone who hears the call of the rebel in their blood is worthy to walk this path. There is no gatekeeping, there is no one true path. There is simply immersing yourself into the mystery of life and acknowledging yourself as a sacred being, flaws, mistakes, and all.

If there is one mantra I might offer to you, seeker, it is this: "I am enough." Write that on your mirror in red lipstick, tattoo it on your chest, or sing it from the rooftops. For truly, right now, in this moment, you are enough.

The one rule for this path is for you to *own* that you walk this path. You owe explanations to no one. You get to call the shots and make the decisions. You get to make the glorious mistakes. You get to celebrate the amazing successes. Just you.

You get to be your own spiritual authority. Welcome to the path of the rebel.

Toxic Positivity

Women are conditioned to be nice, and these messages don't end during childhood. The messages of toxic positivity and conformity also come through when we are encouraged by others to shake it off, just smile, focus on the positive, or only take in the good vibes. As if there is some secret formula to just get over abuse, terror, violence, suppression, oppression, and lies! No, not really. Ignored behavior does not change the behavior.

As I kid, I was told to ignore the boy who bullied me. When he teased me, kicked my chair while I was trying to concentrate, followed me home yelling taunts, and said cruel and ugly things, I was expected to just ignore it, be a better person, take the high road. People said he would stop if I just ignored him. I tried that, and he didn't stop.

It didn't work then, and it doesn't work now. That little girl I used to be was willing to conform. She just wanted to fit in and disappear. The adult I am now is a rebel. I would never ignore bad behavior now.

Women in positions of power or leadership are often called bitches, pushy, or worse. Women who act or perform at the same levels as men aren't given the same levels of respect as their male counterparts. Although this is no longer a secret, it's not like awareness has stopped it from happening.

Men who don't fit a particular masculine mold are referred to as being a "pussy" or weak. Being effeminate is still something to avoid in mainstream culture. A man behaving like a woman is considered embarrassing. So embarrassing, in fact, that referring to a man with a slang word for a female's genitals is a derogatory statement. Why would that be?

For folks who don't fall on one end or the other of the gender spectrum, it gets even worse. What happens when none of the labels fit? What happens when you are told over and over again to pick a label, stick to a side, conform, conform, conform. "It's not me that is uncomfortable, I just want life to be easier for you …"

And it doesn't end with gender politics and binary shenanigans either.

Take a look at the messages that come out of the so-called "spiritual" world. You'll be bombarded with messages about taking the high road, offering love to those that have wronged you, and holding forgiveness in your heart. There is a movement of "white light," which means offering any situation white light to raise its vibrational level. Not only is this a watering down of spiritual pursuits, but it's also inherently racist and utter bullshit.

You might be asking, "Why is that racist?" It comes down to a simple answer. According to that ideology, *white* is good, high vibration, and better, whereas *black* or *dark* are bad, low vibration, and lacking. Neither of these things are true.

These are all ways that toxic positivity manifests.

Add to this social media.

Social media allows people to create a positive persona filled with filtered images, cute hashtags, and just the right message for their followers to see how perfect and wonderful their life is. *Good vibes only. Everything happens for a reason. Raise up your vibration.* Just like that phrase from Mary Poppins, "Practically perfect in every way." Barf.

Honey, nothing in the world is perfect. When you only focus on the so-called bright side, you miss half of life. That's not only boring, but it also shuts you down spiritually and emotionally. I call this *white lighting.* It takes the power away from the truth. Light isn't positive and dark isn't negative. Both are necessary and both can be toxic. They need each other to create balance, awareness, and power. True witches and heretics know this. They use this to manifest change.

When you sugarcoat life and only focus on the positive, it creates a false narrative that any challenge or hardship is bad or created by some fault you possess. Toxic positivity leads to the belief that you deserve the abuse because you weren't smiling enough, or being positive enough, or raising your vibration enough; by the Law of Attraction, you manifested that negativity, oppression, and pain. Nope, sorry. I call BS.

Life is filled with peaks and valleys. It is what you do with these moments that is the most important thing. Honor the valley, honor the peak, and honor yourself for going through the process.

Forcing everything into a positive mindset isn't necessary. You don't have to be nice or sweet. You don't have to forgive those who have wronged you. You don't have to pretend like you are okay when you're not. The time of toxic positivity needs to come to an end.

WITCH WOUND

Imagine a widowed old woman living alone at the edge of the woods or just outside the village. She's poor but does her best to get by. Maybe she's able to help midwife birthing mothers, maybe she knows a bit about herbal remedies, but she's a bit on the outskirts of the social norms.

At some point there's a tragedy in the village. Perhaps there's a drought or a blight on the crops one year. Perhaps a pregnant woman and her child die during childbirth. Perhaps a sick cow stops giving milk. Tragedy strikes and often people look for a scapegoat. (Society still does this today. We love our scapegoats!) Who better to serve as that scapegoat than the outsider? She becomes the easy sacrifice. She can take the blame and really, who will miss her? No one. She becomes the witch, the heretic.

If you are weird, if you are different, if you don't fit in with the majority, you run the risk of being called out. And as we can see from history, being called out can literally kill you. Witches and people who were different were burned at the stake. This sent the following messages: Don't stand out. Don't be seen as someone outside the norm. Follow the crowd and keep your head down. Don't be a witch. Don't be a heretic. Just don't.

Being labeled a witch and hunted for it isn't something that only happened in the 1500s or during the witch trials; it still happens now. And I'm not talking about when modern folks throw the term "witch hunt" about.

For our ancestors, the literal accusation of witchcraft came with a hefty price. And it's a price many of us are still paying. Part of that price is the Witch Wound. The Witch Wound is a piece of ancestral trauma many us of carry. This wound affects women and/or queer, trans, or gender-fluid folks more than others. It is held in our bodies, in our spirits, and in the energy of the cultures we were born into. It stems from the real trauma experienced by our ancestors. And from a culture that wants us to conform.

We are the descendants of that wounding. Our culture is a descendant of that wounding. Colonization and conformity are symptoms of the Witch Wound in the overculture we all live in. No group can claim origination of the Witch Wound. It lives in our world, all around us. Even if you're not a witch, you are impacted by that wound. Patriarchy created that wound.

In Australia, there is a saying: "Don't be a tall poppy or you'll be the first cut down." (It's a saying in other parts of the world too, but I learned it there.) The idea being that if you're too big, too tall, too much—if you stand out more than the rest of the flowers—you'll be torn down. This is easy to see manifested in real life, especially if you've been involved with any larger spiritual communities or taken on leadership in any community. Tall poppy syndrome is a symptom of the Witch Wound.

There is a phenomenon of lifting people up and encouraging them to become leaders, but only to a certain point. Once someone reaches a certain level of fame, success, or notoriety, once someone outgrows what others perceive as "their place," they are torn down by the very same people who helped them rise into leadership in the first place. Another term for this is *eating your own.*

If you are reading this book, you're likely already taking the steps to heal your Witch Wound, whether consciously or unconsciously. But in case you aren't sure, here are some ways that the Witch Wound expresses itself, both in ourselves and in our communities:

- Feeling alone and without community or like-minded people
- Disconnection from your ancestral wisdom and lineage
- Being or feeling disembodied
- Suppressing your emotions or true feelings; going along to get along
- Fear of being seen and/or being motivated by a desire to be seen
- Disconnection from your intuitive self
- Mistrust or distrust of others
- Suppressing your personal power

If you are working on healing your personal Witch Wound, you may have already faced some of these issues, or you may at least be familiar with these ideas. If this is a new concept for you, these bullet points might bring up an emotional reaction or an aha moment.

The Witch Wound easily festers. Its infection tells us we are alone. It doesn't matter your ancestry, gender, sexual orientation, age, faith, race, or upbringing, this wound impacts us all. It is strengthened by fundamentalism, patriarchy, and capitalism. The cultural disconnection to the mysteries of the natural world only deepens this wound.

Remember, most modern witches are healers—emotional, spiritual, herbal, and so on. These collective wounds can be cleansed and healed. The scars left behind serve as a reminder of all we have successfully changed. The scars left behind are badges of honor showing us the warriors we are. It's time to reconnect and strengthen our place in the web of life. Each of us is a unique and beautiful strand. We were born to glow, sing, and thrum with our own personal power.

Working through this book, I encourage you to be the tall poppy. Stand up and stand out. Face your Witch Wound, cleanse it, take care of it, and let it start to heal.

The Devil, Lucifer, or Morningstar

It is impossible to delve into the world of the rebel without addressing the Devil. Hello, Devil! In the purest definition of the word *heretic*, which is a big part of being a rebel, anyone accused of heresy was believed to be in league with the Devil and evil incarnate. How can we discuss being a rebel and a heretic without addressing the giant, evil demon in the room?

But seriously, most of us, whether Christian or not, have been deeply influenced by Christianity. It is overwhelmingly part of the mainstream. I was not raised in a specific religion; there was no Bible camp or church on Sundays in my childhood. But we did celebrate Easter and Christmas in secular ways. There was, and always has been, a cultural assumption from others that I believe in the Christian God or Jesus. Although I didn't go to Bible school, I do know quite a few of the basic stories. And I can sing virtually all the Christian Christmas music. It's pretty mainstream! So, whether or not you were influenced by a Christian church, the culture we live in has been, especially for those of us that live in North America.

Over the years, anyone who went against the cultural belief in Christianity would have been marked as a heretic. That is no less true today.

The connection between rebellious thinking, witchcraft, and the Devil is a simple history lesson in control and religious domination. When you want to control a population, you have to take away their beliefs, show them what they are doing is evil, and frighten them into believing in an eternal hell for being wrong. You don't want to suffer forever in hell, do you?

There are lots of books and papers written about the *devilization* of many Pagan gods, and we aren't going to go into all of that here. However, it's pretty common knowledge that deities of the forest, of sex, of pleasure, and of the wild from many cultures were demonized, and their likenesses were often connected to images and actions of the Christian Devil.

We don't have time to go deep into Christian theology, but suffice it to say that the Devil has always been a counterpart of God. His story is one that evolved as the church evolved. The way he showed up in the world changed as the circumstances of power and domination changed.

In later stories, Lucifer and the Devil and Satan become conflated. Lucifer the fallen angel, who loved God so much he was stripped of his beauty and power because of it, started being compared with this concept of the Devil, or original evil. Lucifer became one of the faces of the Devil or Satan.

Many modern witches have found a soft spot for the fallen angel, calling upon him as Dark Lord or Lord of the Witches. His story is a rather romantic one. He was so in love with his God that he was punished for all eternity for putting Him above all others. In some ways this entity has evolved into a leader for witches in modern times, but it cannot be missed that his origins were that of Judaism and then more intensely in Christianity.

You can find plenty of witchcraft traditions, heretical in their own right, who work with Lucifer the Morningstar, the rebel. They call upon the Dark Lord, the Devil, or the man at the cross-roads in their spiritual workings. But this is not the truth for all witches or all heretics.

If the thought of calling upon the Devil, Lucifer, or Morning star makes your skin crawl and has you rethinking the path of the rebel, don't worry. There is no dark book to sign, no midnight mass you must participate in. The Devil isn't part of *my* heretical nature. He doesn't play into my witchcraft, and he doesn't have to be a part of yours either. He is mentioned here only because of his connection to the history of the word *heretic*, and it is not a modern requirement to have a relationship with him in order to be one.

PART TWO

BEING THE WITCH

Chapter 4
The Witches

What comes up for you when you see the word *witch*? Does your mind go to the classic images of the scary old woman making potions over a cauldron? Maybe you see the evil stepmother from Snow White. Or perhaps you think of an overly sexualized beautiful woman, a vixen who will lure you into her bed. Could be that your thoughts go to the witchcraft aesthetic that's so popular on social media: young people burning herbs in cauldrons, wearing hats, with tattooed fingers, pointed black nails, and flowy black dresses.

It doesn't really matter what image your imagination conjures up when you read the word *witch*. The word still packs a punch in mainstream society. For folks who don't walk in alternative worlds, calling yourself a witch can be met with fear, scorn, mockery, or worse.

I've called myself a witch for close to thirty years. I've received all the reactions. From being asked to cast a spell, to outright mocking laughter, to a family member who worried about my immortal soul and said they would pray for me. Taking on the moniker of witch opens you up to a potential world of backlash. And I gotta tell you, babe, that's what it is all about.

Back in the day, the ancestors who we might consider witches probably didn't call themselves by that word. However, they could be identified in other ways. They may have lived on the fringes of society. They likely lived alone. They may have been eccentric or odd. They were often avoided because they made people uncomfortable or forced them to look at things outside the norm. Thus, the people who knew how to use herbs to heal, help birth babies, and make things happen were often those accused of being witches. These were the people who were revered from a place of fear by the mainstream. They were ostracized when things were going smooth and easy but called upon when the shit hit the fan.

This is still the case.

Times have changed, but calling yourself a witch is still controversial. You may live in a progressive bubble like I have the good fortune to do, but that's not the case for all of us. Owning your witch title is an act of derision; it is spitting in the face of our overculture. It is a giant middle finger to the mundane. It is an act that is dangerous and brave. And it is not to be taken on lightly.

So, you wanna be a witch? Great! I fully support you. But I want you to know that this path asks you to be strong, bold, and relentless in doing your work in the world. There are no half measures in witchcraft. There is no dabbling in this stuff; dabbling is disrespectful. Do it or don't, but don't tiptoe around the power. Grab it by the horns, leap on its back, and ride it into the sunset.

And conversely, because we rebels love paradox, you can totally claim the title of witch and not wear it like a glowing neon sign for the world to see. To be a witch is personal and private. It is *your* journey. Don't feel like you have to literally put yourself in danger in order to be a witch. There are many places in the world where that label could cause you physical harm. Be safe and be careful. A witch is nothing if not smart. If your life doesn't make it safe for you to ride your broom into the office, then wear that title in your heart and not on your sleeve.

THE BROOM

The tool of the witch is the broom. Witches and brooms go together like peanut butter and jelly. Witches travel on their brooms. They take a simple household item and use it to fly. It's a skill of the supernatural to defy the laws of physics and gravity. Sounds amazing and fun, doesn't it?

Here's the bad news: I don't know anyone that literally flies on a broom. I know, it's a bummer. However, the broom is a classic tool that has been associated with witches for hundreds of years. There is a folklore from all over the world connected to brooms. For example:

- If a broom falls, company is coming.
- Leave an old broom behind when you move houses to leave your "dirt" behind as well.
- Store your broom with the bristles up for good luck.
- Don't let anyone borrow your broom or they could steal your luck.
- Don't sweep over another person's feet or you could bring about their death.

One act of witchcraft is to hang a broom above your front door. This will help you out twofold. For one thing, it helps to keep *out* people and energies that are unwanted, and two, it helps to keep *in* positive energy and abundance.

Creating Your Own Simple Broom

The following broom-making ideas are for a magickal decorative broom. This broom should be hung in your home and should not be used for cleaning.

The first step in creating your own broom is to choose the wood for your handle. There are lots of different options, but you will want a piece of wood that comes up at least to your waist when resting on the floor. Ideally, the wood you choose would be naturally harvested, but not all trees grow in all places. If you can't find the wood you want locally, it is totally okay to purchase it from a shop or online. Take your time finding a piece of wood with the energy that will match your goals for this broom.

CHOOSING YOUR HANDLE

Here are some basics about wood energy:

- **Alder:** Wood from an alder tree is most often connected to more watery workings. The wood will turn red after being cut, so it is often used in connection to the menstrual cycle or blood magick. It is a wood of strength, passion, and endurance.

- **Apple:** Apple wood is a traditional favorite for wand making, which means it will also work well as a broom handle. Apple wood is connected to love. It is a wood of beauty and generosity.

- **Ash:** This type of wood is very popular for creating a broom. This tree is connected to Yggdrasil, or the world tree, in Norse mythology. It is a very magickal wood. It is a wood of connection, surrender, and wisdom.

- **Birch:** Most often, birch twigs are used to make the ends or bristles of the broom, but the wood is also excellent for creating the broom handle. It is a wood of purity, healing, and banishing.
- **Elder:** The elder tree has a long history of being connected to witches. It stands as a portal between the realms. It is a wood of banishing, purification, and magick.
- **Elm:** Elm trees are traditionally used as the wood for maypoles. This gives the elm tree association with love and love magick. It is a wood of relationship, love, and witches.
- **Maple:** This type of tree has a sturdy, strong wood that is often used to make magickal objects. It is a wood of industry, abundance, and prosperity.
- **Oak:** Oak trees are revered in many cultures. The wood of this tree is used for protection, power, and stability.
- **Pine:** The brooms you find at most mainstream stores are likely made with a pine wood handle. They are study and dependable. A wood for healing, fertility, and prosperity.
- **Rowan:** This type of tree has long been associated with witches, often used as protection against them. It is a highly protective wood, good for connection and expression.
- **Walnut:** The wood from a walnut tree is strong. It comes with long, folkloric history of witches being found in walnut forests. This wood is good for prosperity, healing, and luck.

CHOOSING YOUR BRUSH

Once you have picked out your handle, it's time to pick out your brush. Traditionally you would use broom straw, but you can select any number of herbs that might be in alignment with the energy that you want your broom to hold. Brushes are best when made out of strong, thick, and sturdy dried materials. Plants that whither rather than dry out don't work well because they don't hold their form. A broom brush made of pansies would be pretty to look at, but only for a moment. As soon as the plants whither, it's useless. For your brush, stick with hardy herbs, plants, or small twigs.

- **Birch Twigs:** In folk traditions, birch has been used as a tool for striking out negative entities—literally. Hitting people with the branches was a form of exorcism. It is also used to repel the evil eye.
- **Broom Straw:** This plant is used as a tool for purification and protection. It can help to clear negative energies and negative spirits.
- **Cedar:** Boughs of cedar are used to protect against evil. It can also be used to call in love and financial prosperity.
- **Lavender:** Dried lavender is used to help maintain peaceful energy. The flowers are used to help alleviate depression and bring longevity.
- **Pine Needles:** The needles from a pine tree repel negative energy and illness. It's also used to call in financial prosperity and joy.
- **Rosemary:** Rosemary is used to keep away bad dreams and call in good ones. In folk traditions, it keeps thieves away from the home and ensures protection for those inside.

PUTTING IT TOGETHER

To create your broom, simply bind your chosen brush to the bottom edge of the wooden handle. Hold the herbs firmly around the bottom piece of wood and wrap them as snugly as you can on the handle. Right when you think you're done, wrap a bit more. Then attach your brush to your broom handle; raffia, yarn, willow branches, and vine all work well.

Once your broom is assembled you can paint it, carve into the handle, and/or anoint it with oils or magickal blends. When it's all finished, lay it on a windowsill and charge it under the full moon. If you work with a specific deity, ask for their blessing on your magickal tool.

Hang your broom above your front door, above your altar, or overlooking any magickal space.

✦ ✦ ✦ Personal Contemplation ✦ ✦ ✦

Do you feel like a witch? Do you already consider yourself one, or is this a new idea? How do you imagine witchcraft will change your life?

Take out your journal and write the word WITCH across the top of the page. Set a timer for five minutes and free write on this word. Anything and everything that comes up is fair game.

When the timer goes off, set your journal aside for at least one full day. When you feel ready, read over what you've written. How does it make you feel?

Then write the words I AM A WITCH on the top of a new page. Set a timer for five minutes and free write on what comes up for you with this statement.

When the timer goes off, set your journal aside for at least one full day. When you are ready, read over what you've written. How does it make you feel? Are you ready to call yourself a witch?

Witches of This Book

There are hundreds of witches that could have been a part of this book. So many, in fact, that it was super hard for me to choose just three. But choose I did. Selecting these powerful witches does not undermine the power of any witch not selected.

In the following chapters, we will explore the lives and energies of three famous witches: Circe, Anne Boleyn, and Marie Laveau. You will have the opportunity to learn more about each of their lives and connect with their power.

With that, let's be on our way ...

CHAPTER 5
CIRCE

The witch known as Circe (pronounced seer-see or sir-see) comes to us from Greek mythology. She is the only mythological woman selected for this book. Circe lived alone on an island called Aeaea (pronounced i-A-ah) and featured in the story of Odysseus, written by Homer. She was known to be a witch and was both revered and feared for her magick. Her story feels so very human, and she is the ultimate witch icon.

Circe is the daughter of the Titan Helios and an ocean nymph called Perse. This is actually an important relationship that isn't given much focus in the writings about Circe. Her father was the sun personified; her mother was one of thousands of ocean nymphs who caught the eye of the sun god. Helios was one of the Old Godds, and he became an outcast when Zeus and the Olympians came into power.[3]

---

3. Note: I use the spelling of *godds* as a more gender-neutral way of spelling the word. You will see me use this word when speaking generally of godds or for a godd that is genderfull or fluid. If I am speaking of a deity with a clear binary gender, I will use god or goddess as appropriate.

Why is this something to note? Well, the Titans were the Old Godds. They were connected to the forces of nature. I'll take that one step further—they *were* the forces of nature. In the mythologies, Zeus is born and locks the Titans away. He is a son of the Titans, but he supplants them and becomes ruler himself.

This change from Titan, wild, natural energies to Olympian-controlled rulers is a reflection of a major culture shift. The mythology suggests that during the time of the Titan's rule, humans were more connected to the earth and the forces of nature. Then there is a shift, a major cultural change, and the "world" moves to a more patriarchal focus. Culture went from worshipping or honoring (perhaps even fearing) the forces of nature to revering a "sky father" and his kin. The sky father who dominates the forces of nature. This shift didn't happen overnight, but happen it did and we are *still* living in a culture that is based on that shift.

Circe is a child of the Old Godds. When culture shifted, so did how she was viewed. A demigod with magickal powers turned into a dangerous witch. She became a terrifying, banished woman, living alone on an island. Her only means of connection came from tricking men into staying with her through the use of her potions and magick wand.

What might the story of Circe have looked like if not told through the lens of patriarchal culture? This is something that only our imaginations can determine.

She is mentioned in *The Odyssey*, written by Homer in the eighth century BCE. This story is the journey of the hero Odysseus, a man who became lost at sea with his crew after fighting in the war. As they try to find their way home, they encounter island after island of sometimes helpful, sometimes harmful characters. At one point, Odysseus and his men stumble upon Circe's island of Aeaea.

Some believe the story of *The Odyssey*, although written down by Homer, was actually part of a much older oral tradition. What might Circe have been like in those tales? When a myth goes from oral tradition to written legend, it becomes frozen in the time it was written down. We lose nuance and context. I'm also a believer in the theory that many of the Greek tales that have been written down were the fan fiction of their time. Popular writers would write fantastical tales as a way to honor the godds, and Homer was one of the more popular writers. However, Homer was a product of his time, and many of his tales are rife with patriarchal themes and female suppression. Including the story of Odysseus and his encounter with Circe.

The Odyssey is where we learn the most about this character from Greek myth: "Circe the nymph with lovely braids, an awesome power too who can speak with human voice … Deep inside they heard her singing, lifting her spellbinding voice as she glided back and forth at her great immortal loom, her enchanting web a shimmering glory only goddesses can weave."[4]

In all the writings about her throughout time, Circe is often referred to as a sorceress because she is able to change men into animals using the aid of plant allies. She would use the herbs that grew on her island to make fantastical potions. With a drop of potion in a man's drink, a wave of her wand, and the right enchantment, she could turn men into wolves, lions, birds, and pigs. She knew the magick of potions and used them upon those that came to visit her—for good or ill.

When the men from Odysseus's ship went to explore the island of Aeaea, at first without Odysseus, they were rude and crass. The sorceress was able to tell that they had lust in their

---

4. Homer, *The Odyssey*, 234, 237.

hearts. Knowing that she could not trust these wayward men, she offered them food and drink and turned them into pigs. Only one sailor remained unturned, and he ran back to warn the rest of his shipmates of what had happened.

Odysseus, as their leader, headed to her simple home on the island. Before reaching her, he was confronted by one of his spiritual allies, Hermes, who told him he could avoid the impact of Circe's potions by using an herb called moly.

When Odysseus avoided being turned into a pig, this shocked the goddess. But even with the use of Hermes's magickal herb, Odysseus was still "enthralled" to stay on Circe's island for a year. If you read the tales, you might imagine that Circe manipulated Odysseus with incantations, potions, and magick. But if you read between the lines—if you take the story a bit deeper—you can see that she held a thread of magick that was actually aiding the tired sailor.

In Circe's halls, the traveler finally found a bit of peace, respite, and rest after a terrible war and being lost at sea for years. Odysseus was comforted, and so were his men—once Circe turned them back into humans. They were well fed and cared for. Odysseus lay in the goddess's bed every night. And it was only after a *year*, when his men started to hound him about returning home, that Odysseus started to feel uneasy about the situation he had lucked into.

When Odysseus decided to leave, Circe didn't force him to stay. She didn't further bind him with spells. Rather, she gave him the key to returning home after being lost at sea for so long. She told him that he needed to complete an important ritual that could only take place in the Underworld. Without Circe's wisdom and advice, Odysseus and his men would never have been able to find their way home.

Circe has been written about for thousands of years, up to present day. By looking at her stories over time, we can see how (mostly male) writers have demonized this powerful woman. Her story shifts from her being a goddess, to a sorceress, to a prostitute, to a witch. A threat to all things masculine. Circe shifts from a self-contained power to a danger to men. Not an unfamiliar journey for many a powerful spirit in history and mystery.

Even in the oldest stories, the message is clear: Women who are self-possessed, who know the power of potions, who understand the magick of plants, and who use magick to aid those they love, are cast as wicked.

What's a witch to do? Well, I'll tell ya. Embrace it!

That's right. Own your power. Learn the lore of plants, especially the ones that grow where you live. Take a course, go online, read books on herbology. Understand the medicine and the magick of the green bloods. Support your family and friends with this knowledge.

Be the witch. Call upon your witch ancestors, both of blood and of magick. Get yourself a broom. Get yourself a wand. Cast magickal circles. Use that magickal tool to bless, charge, and consecrate your workings.

Does the idea of having a wand make you feel a little silly or childish? Good! Go with that. Embracing your inner witch is serious business, but it should also be filled with mirth, joy, fun, and wonder. The best magick calls to our child selves. We have to engage in play in order for our magick to be successful. Our child selves must be on board with our witchcraft. Be silly, act a fool, and wave a wand around your kitchen, blessing and enchanting everything you touch. Be the witch!

Of Wands and Potions

We know from the stories that Circe's magick was connected to the potions she created using the plants on her island as well as her magickal wand. She gave the sailors a potion mixed with a drink. Not suspecting anything was amiss, they drank, and Circe activated the magick in the potion using her wand, turning them into pigs. The wand is what activated the power of the potion. It was the final stamp in her spell, the catalyst, the source of her power.

From this, we can determine two things. A potion is just a mixture of plants, liquid, and other magickal bits, but it is the power of the witch in her *activation* of those ingredients that creates the magick. Therefore, we too can harness that energy. Know the magick of the plants, learn your herblore and herbology, but don't forget to make it a potion by adding the right magickal energy.

Wands

All witches need a wand. It is tool of directing power. The wand helps you focus on your goal, call in the energy you need, and direct it in a concentrated form. Think of a wand like an arrow; you focus on the goal and then shoot out your energy to hit it. The wand is what moves your energy from here to there.

Traditionally, a witch's wand is the length of her arm from the elbow to the tip of her middle finger. Again, traditionally, they are made from natural materials, most often wood. If you decide to create a wand from wood, look back at chapter 4's section on brooms and wood handles. This same information can be translated into wand usage. However, modern witches have been known to make wands out of metal, clay, glass, crystal, animal bone, and any other thing you can imagine.

Once you have your wand, you can decorate it. Carve symbols, sigils, or letters into it. Anoint it with oils. Attach stones to it, either with wire or hot glue. Make it into a magickal object that brings you delight.

When you use your wand, you should hold it in your dominant hand. Your dominant hand is the directive energetic hand, while your nondominant hand is the receptive energetic hand.

Hold your wand in your dominant hand, take a deep breath, and feel (or perhaps imagine) energy running through you. Whether you realize it or not, you have energy running through your body all the time. Electrical currents move through your body and help keep you alive. You can tap into that energy and use it for magick. Visualize that energy gathering up into a ball of glowing light in your center. Direct that ball of energy down your dominant arm, then use your wand to direct it out of you and toward something else.

How was that? Try it again. And then again. Keep practicing until it feels totally easy and normal.

The good news is wands are super easy to find. You don't have to go out and purchase anything fancy or wander into the dark wood at midnight on a full moon to collect the wood from a tree that was hit by lightning. I mean, you totally *can* do all these things; it is fun to go into the woods late at night and find a cool tree. But we are all born with wands. Hold out the first two fingers on your dominant hand. Voilà! Wand!

USE A WAND FOR:
- Directing energy
- Charging objects with power
- Making a boundary
- Casting a circle
- Working with spirits
- Sending messages
- Blessing spells or potions
- Energetically drawing sigils, wards, or runes

Potions

Officially, a potion is just a liquid with healing, magickal, or poisonous properties. That's a pretty broad definition. This suggests that virtually anything can be made into a potion. Do you drink peppermint tea when you have a stomachache? Well, that's a potion. Do you take an immune tincture in the winter to help you stay healthy? Potion! Do you make chicken noodle soup for your loved ones when they are ill? Yup, that's a potion too!

What changes something from a healing tincture, bowl of soup, or cup of tea into something more powerful is the intent and magickal activation.

The intent comes at the very start of the process. When you begin gathering ingredients, focus on your ultimate goal for them. Hold that in your heart and mind. Focus your will on what those ingredients need to do for you. With each step of the process, hold that energy in your consciousness. It doesn't matter if you are wildcrafting the herbs, picking them from your yard, or buying them at a store, the importance comes from your intent.

MAKING AN ANOINTING POTION

This is an exercise in fun, frivolity, and practical potion making. The goal is to feel magickal, be silly, engage your child self, and make some magick all at the same time. Although this ritual may be silly, the power of it is intensely serious and could easily be transferred to a potion for anything else. This ritual should be done in your kitchen. Remember, the intention of this working is play and joyful energy—focus on that as you move through the steps.

1. Go to the spice cabinet in your home and open the door or put your spice rack in a place where you can easily see what you've got.

2. Get out a cooking pot and place it on the stove.

3. Put liquid into your pot. This could be water or anything else your gut tells you to use, but it should be something that won't harm you and is safe to put on your skin.

4. Start putting in spices. Don't worry about the magickal alignment of these spices or what they could be used for. This is a practice of play. Read the label, take a sniff, and decide whether it goes into the pot or not. Remember, this is a mixture for anointing, so don't use anything that might irritate your skin (like cayenne pepper, for example).

5. Keep going until your intuition tells you your potion is done. There should be enough herbs and spices that you can see something is happening in that pot.

6. Turn on the stove and bring your mixture to a nice boil.

7. Cackle, chant, tone, or sing over the potion as it bubbles away on the stove. Recite "Double, double toil and trouble." Maybe dance a little bit? C'mon, really go for it.

8. Turn off the stove and let the potion cool while you dance around the kitchen, clapping your hands in witchy delight over the spell you're working.

9. Put your potion into a jar. Store it in a cool, dry place. It will keep for up to a week. If you want it to keep longer, add alcohol, which will keep it usable for months.

Use this potion anytime you need to awaken your child self, invoke play, or have fun. DON'T DRINK THIS POTION. Use it for external anointing purposes only.

Walking Between the Worlds

Witches know how to travel between the realms. There is more to the world than what we can see with our regular eyes. There are worlds right next to this one that we can connect with, commune with, and learn from. Circe knew this.

We know from her mythology that Circe was a demigod, so of course she understood there are many worlds. But even the godds are not all capable of moving from one realm into the next. This is serious, difficult magick.

In *The Odyssey*, Circe tells Odysseus that he must go to the Underworld if he ever wants to return to his homeland.[5] This is not a feat easily performed; mortals are not allowed to go to the Underworld and then simply leave. But Circe knows the way, and she tells Odysseus exactly what he must do and how he must do it. She gives him all the tools he will need for his success.

Because Circe knows the ways of traveling between the worlds, she is also able to tell Odysseus everything he needs to do to complete an impossible journey: "Dig a trench of about a

---

5. Homer, *The Odyssey*, 246.

forearms depth and length and around it, pour libations out to all the dead—first with milk and honey, and then with mellow wine, then water third and last, and sprinkle glistening barley over it all, and vow again to all the dead ..."[6]

Based on Circe's guidance, Odysseus not only made it to the Underworld, completed the tasks set before him, and dealt with some personal demons, but he also made it back unscathed.

His fear was intense, but he carried on with the blessing of his lover, the witch, Circe. He faced his demons and confronted the shadows that had been hidden from his consciousness. It was only then that he was able to make his way "home."

Look at this story as a parable for facing your own wounds and triggers. The journey is perilous and filled with fear. But when we honor our inner witch and listen to her wisdom, we will hold in our hands the glowing light that we can shine on our hidden shadows and reveal their truths. When we make this journey and do the work of owning all our parts, we can again return to our internal home stronger and wiser.

Walking between the worlds is a practice of connecting with your own hidden shadows and bright shadows. It is a practice of knowing yourself. When you travel between the realms— between the worlds—you gather valuable information about yourself that you might otherwise not know.

With the right guides and preparation, you could travel to the Underworld, to the Otherworlds, and to the other realms. You could fact find to fill in the gaps of your own awareness.

---

6. Homer, *The Odyssey*, 246.

⟨◈⟩ Traveling to the Realm of Circe ⟨◈⟩

This working is best done near the ocean or a body of water. If that isn't possible for you, try to be outside in as wild a place as you can be.

Supplies: A cup of herbal tea of your choice (in a thermos is best), your wand, and a blanket or chair to sit on.

Set Up: Set up your space to allow you to be as physically comfortable as possible. For this working, you will be going on a trance. You may want to lay down on a blanket, cushion, or reclined chair. Once this is set up, put out your wand and cup of tea. Get comfortable, holding your wand in your hands.

Trance: Let yourself be as comfortable as possible and breathe deeply and slowly. Take some time to feel the gentle inhalation and exhalation of your breath. Notice how your lungs fill with air and how this process cycles your blood, keeping you alive. Take a moment to feel gratitude for this process that happens without you having to think about it.

As you breathe, notice a soft, warm light surrounding your toes. This light relaxes and releases everything it touches. All your cells, muscles, tendons, and bones are relaxed as this warm glow touches them. Continue your breathing, and as you do, the light grows, traveling up your feet and swirling around your ankles.

With each breath the light moves upward, relaxing and releasing every bit of you it touches. It moves up your shins and calves, surrounding you in a warm glow. The light continues moving up around your knees, thighs, and hips; it is warm and relaxing. The light fills your pelvic bowl and belly. It moves up your spine and around your ribs. It leaves every cell, muscle, tendon, and bone relaxed.

This warm glow moves across your chest, around your shoulders and arms, and shoots out of each fingertip. This light allows you to be deeply relaxed, calm, and safe. The glow swirls around your neck and ears, down your jawline, around your eyes, and over your forehead, leaving all of you covered in the warm, relaxing glow.

Finally, that light of relaxation swirls around the top of your head, coming to a close. Your whole body is now covered in a warm glow that keeps you deeply relaxed. From this place you are able to open your third eye—your witch's eye—the one that sits just above and between your normal seeing eyes.

When your witch's eye opens, you see before you a path. In the distance you hear the soft lap of waves on a sandy shoreline and you taste the brine on the air. You follow the path, putting one foot in front of the other, step by step, moving toward the sound of water.

As you walk along the path, notice any animals or plants that may make themselves known to you. As you walk along this path, one foot in front of the other, notice what sounds or smells you may pick up.

You reach an opening, and before you there is a vast expanse of shoreline. A calm, crystal-clear ocean is lapping against a white sandy beach. And bobbing along in the water is a boat. Step into the boat. (Pause.)

As soon as you are secure in the boat, it begins to move. Gently rocking in the lapping waves, the boat moves with an unseen force. You move forward, ever closer to a small island in the distance. You can feel the soft spray of salty ocean on your face and hear the call of sea birds around you. The boat moves swiftly, carrying you ever closer to the tree-covered island. (Pause.)

The boat finally scrapes along the sandy shoreline of Aeaea, Circe's island, and comes to a stop. You leave the boat and see a path leading from the shoreline into the trees. You follow along the path, moving ever closer to the heart of the island. As you walk through the trees, you can smell the faint scent of wood-smoke on the air.

You come to an opening in the trees with a beautiful house in the center of the clearing. The doors open and Circe walks out. She welcomes you to her home and island. Take some time to speak with her and find out what wisdom she holds for you as you follow the path of the witch. (Long pause.)

Ask Circe if she is willing to bless the wand you hold in your hands. Ask for some of her wisdom and skill to pass from her hands into your wand. (Long pause.)

Your time on Circe's island is limited, but know that you can return here at any time. For now, ask any last questions you may hold in your heart. (Long pause.)

If you haven't already, take some time to say goodbye and offer your gratitude to Circe. When you are ready, turn and move away from the house in the woods, going back to the path that brought you here. You move quickly, following the path back to the shoreline where your boat awaits you. (Pause.)

You get onboard the boat and it moves away from the shore-line. The boat gently rocks you, moving silently over the waves. The water is clear and calm, and you can see the shore where you began your journey in the distance. The boat moves swiftly, and you quickly find yourself returned to your starting point.

You disembark the boat, returning to the path that brought you here. Your feet find their way along the path, leading you back to your body. Take a step and then another, placing one foot in front of the other along the path home.

As you move along, take note of your breathing. As you take note of your breathing, allow your witch's eye to close. As that eye closes, breathe deeply and fully, feeling the edges of your body. Allow those edges to become firm. Call them in with each inhale. (Pause.)

Take note of the edges of your body. Use the palm of your hands to tap the edges of your form, your legs, arms, and the top of your head. When you feel ready, slowly open your eyes. If you have been laying down, slowly sit up. Stretch your arms and yawn. Speak your name out loud three times.

Welcome back!

Set down your wand. Pour out some of your tea as an offering to Circe and drink some. Allow yourself time to drink the tea and enjoy your surroundings. Contemplate anything that came up for you during your journey.

BEING A WITCH WITH CIRCE

Circe can show us how to embrace our personal power. Yes, she understands the magick of plants and spellcrafting, but her spells are successful because of her personal power. If you take on a magickal working, spell, or even a big goal for your life, you have a much better chance of success when you have faith and trust in yourself and your ability to succeed.

Sure, anyone can follow a pre-written spell, use the herbs, recite the rhyme, and light the candle. And yeah, maybe their spell will be successful. You can totally luck into success. But faith in yourself and your abilities is paramount to any long-term success. You have to believe in what you can accomplish.

Some witches and magickal practitioners have started speaking out against "self-help" practices. There are witches who have even gone as far as saying that type of work isn't witchcraft. Well, I'm here to tell you they are wrong.

Circe shows us that internal personal power *is* witchcraft.

And guess what? You don't achieve self-mastery or personal power if you don't take on the inner work. You need to face your hidden shadows and bring them out into the sun. Witchcraft asks you to understand yourself and your motivations. You have to be willing to dig into your personal programming and figure out the hows and whys of who you are.

This is hard work, but it makes your potions thrum with power.

This is challenging work, but it makes you a badass.

This is the work of the witch.

Circe knows all of this. In fact, I would challenge you to read *The Odyssey*, digging into her part of the story specifically. She showed Odysseus how to vanquish his own demons. She told him the only way he could return home was by facing his hidden shadows.

Only one who has walked that path themselves can help others to do the same. Think about that.

✦ ✦ ✦ Witch Contemplation ✦ ✦ ✦

Where in your life can you see yourself embracing your power like Circe? Write down five places, circumstances, or situations where you have given your power away. How does this make you feel?

Pick one of these situations where you feel ready to reclaim your power. Write down five steps you could take to shift the power dynamic.

Go and take one of these steps now.

CHAPTER 6
ANNE BOLEYN

Anne Boleyn was born to a noble family in England in the early 1500s. For most, being born into a noble family meant living life in search of the crumbs of royal favor. The higher you could go in courtly relationships and connections, the better off you and your family would be. So basically, the pressure was on from birth to kiss ass and try to rise through the ranks of the noble world.

For Anne Boleyn, her father made sure she had the best education possible. At the age of twelve or thirteen, Anne was sent to serve as a maid of honor in the courts of Brussels and later joined the French courts. Because of her life in these European courts and how she was trained and taught by these royals, she returned to her home country different than other English women: "Ever afterwards she would stand out from the women of the English court whom she was leaving, and always would leave, far behind."[7]

---

7. Ives, *Life and Death of Anne Boleyn*, 17.

Anne was greatly influenced by humanist writings during her education. The humanists were some of the first to write about equality and feminism. They believed that common human needs and taking care of each other were of more importance than religious doctrines. These are some pretty heretical ideas now, so imagine how heretical they were in the 1500s!

In 1522 Anne returned to the English court. For the first five years, she was quite the dish and created a bit of a stir. She had many suitors, but her most well-known paramour was King Henry VIII himself. There was only one problem with that: Henry was already married. Henry was so enamored by Anne that he chased off a marriage proposal from another man. That was when the gossip and rumors of Anne and Henry's relationship really took off.

Keep in mind for a courtly woman of the time, a suitable marriage would have been necessary. The right marriage could bring possibility and advantage in status. Losing a marriage proposal from a powerful man was not something that Anne would have wanted. However, she also saw the advantage in Henry being jealous.

Witchcraft is all about using what you've got, and no doubt Anne Boleyn understood this better than anyone.

The relationship between Anne and Henry likely started as most courtly flirtations started. Flirting and the game of seduction was simply a normal part of noble life. But remember, Anne was not like the other English noble women; she was smart and independent. She possessed an allure from being trained in foreign courts that gave her an air the other women could not contend with. All of these things, plus her beguiling nature and the fact that she didn't just give into him, enflamed Henry's passions.

Anne would not be a mistress; she made it clear to Henry that she wanted to be his wife. So, when Henry was unable to get his first marriage annulled through the Catholic church, he was furious. He was king! Who was the church to tell him what to do? Rather than stay married to his first wife, he broke from the Catholic church, forever changing the spiritual landscape of England by forming the Church of England, with the archbishop of Canterbury becoming the most powerful man in the English church.

Henry's first wife was loved by the people and the courtiers, not to mention nobility in other countries. Anne didn't have a lot of support on her side. Some women in these circumstances may have kept a low profile, tried to stay out of any hot-button topics, and avoided attention, but that was not Anne's way. "A different woman might have responded by ignoring the critics and trusting to her own attractions and her ability to nag or persuade the king into marriage, but not Anne Boleyn, she entered politics."[8] Anne had achieved what every person in England would have wanted—royal favor, and from the king himself!

It was obvious to all that Anne was the king's mistress. However, the two maintained a distance from each other and were cautious to keep up appearances of chastity. It wasn't until three *years* after the fight for annulment that Anne and Henry were wed. Nine months after the wedding, Anne gave birth to a healthy baby girl, who would go on to become Queen Elizabeth I. Sadly, the birth of a son would have made her seem more legitimate to the people, and so the birth of a daughter left Anne in a difficult situation: unliked, viewed as a harlot, and with only a female heir. Not good.

---

8. Ives, *Life and Death of Anne Boleyn*, 101.

Anne's intrigue and courtly magick only had the capacity to hold on to Henry's attention for so long. What she had to do was give birth to a son. Unfortunately, Anne continued to have miscarriages. The pressure was on, and when she didn't have a son, Henry started to look for ways to change his fate. The allure she originally had that pulled Henry into her orbit no longer held the same appeal to him. All of the things he initially was smitten by—her involvement in politics, her strong will, and her independence—started to annoy and anger him.

Another woman came on the scene who was willing to do all the demure, quiet, courtly, feminine things that Anne would not. Henry's head easily turned, especially since Anne had still not produced a male heir. At the same time, he started to use the rumors about her against her. The worst of the rumors whispered of treason against Henry. And the king used these rumors as a means for opening an investigation of treason against Anne Boleyn.

She was arrested and tried. Several of the jury members (all men, of course) had political leanings of their own; some were even former paramours of Anne. Sounds like a typical witch trial to me.

This might come as a shock to you, but she was found guilty of treason and beheaded four days after her verdict came down.

Anne Boleyn was whispered about. Gossip and rumors said that she was a witch, but she was never formally accused of witchcraft in the courts. But as you and I both know, all it takes is the right rumor and—true or not—in the public opinion, you are doomed.

The rumors of witchcraft followed Anne to the grave and beyond. She's become an icon of intrigue and an example of how to use power as a tool to gain success and status in the world.

Today, we still see the negative accusation of witchcraft leveled against women. Women are called bitches, pushy, moody, and the age-old favorite, cunts. All these words boil down to the same root, the same fear, the same essence: Women who know what they want and go after it are something to be feared; they are witches.

And truly, even now in this "modern age" when a woman finds success, power, or learns how to wield the tool of intrigue for her own success and advancement, she is painted as a witch, a slut, a whore, a bitch … The list goes on. What is it about a woman owning her power that causes those around her to tremble in fear? Why is a woman something to fear?

This is a question I have pondered since childhood. It's not hard to see the inequalities in the world. We can see this in relation to gender, race, sexuality, religion—anything that creates an "us" versus "them" paradigm. In order to create separation and keep the divide between "us" and "them," those with the most power have to sow seeds of fear about the "other." And that is what the witch is.

Let's pretend, for the sake of mystery, that Anne Boleyn was a witch. Let's go down the rabbit hole of her casting love spells on the hapless king of England. Let's write the story that she had learned the dark arts from various magickal practitioners while living away from the English courts. How about we give Anne the power of a cunning woman, sorceress, and witch.

It's not hard to imagine a courtly woman, dressed in her finery, with sweeping skirts billowing out as she rushes through the stone halls carrying a bowl of herbs mixed with Henry's semen. I can imagine her rushing to the edge of a roaring fireplace with her hair coming unbound and loose around her face. I can see her eyes glowing brightly with otherworldly power (and maybe even a little mischief). Anne Boleyn, the witch.

I can even imagine Anne doing spells to give birth to the greatest monarch England would ever see. For many, Elizabeth I was exactly that. Pretty good spell, even if it is only in my imagination.

OF POWER AND GIFTS

Courtly life is all about power. Anne Boleyn was raised to know this system and to work it to her advantage. She had a desire to rise up the courtly ranks. Her most powerful tools for this task are what made her different: her independence and allure. Anne's gifts became Anne's power, which is ultimately what every courtier, courtesan, prince, king, and squire wants to gain.

Let's be really real here: Power is what every single person on the planet wants to gain. I can already hear some of you folks going, "Nah-uh, not me, I don't care about power." But we all do, and it's not something to be ashamed of or feel bad about. It's just the kinds of power and power seeking that we have to be aware of.

Anne Boleyn was known for her allure. She had a mysterious way of interacting with people. She was smart and educated. Anne understood how she appeared in the world. She knew that women had only a small role to play in courtly society, and she did all she could to make her piece of it as big as possible. She pushed the edges of what society deemed "her place."

She found her power in what made her different, and this is the overall intrigue of Anne Boleyn. She can show us how to utilize these energies in our mundane and magickal lives. Step up and step into the flow of power. Do it!

Power

What is power? Do you feel powerful? Are you afraid of power? Understanding power is a big part of what Anne can teach us. There is power in knowing when to speak and when to stay quiet. Of knowing when to say the flirtatious quip and when to coyly wink an eye.

Although we all want power, many of us also fear it. This is especially true for women. We are taught wanting power is bad and that having power corrupts. The dominant culture we live in has society believing the only way to achieve power is to have power over others. The power-over structure can be seen in governments, corporations, and many structural systems where there are groups and hierarchy. Power can become a tool of oppression. Thanks, patriarchy!

For some of us, power may also bring up fears about anger or violence. Anger and violence are also tools of the patriarchy and another form of power-over relationships. Look at the story of Anne Boleyn as a marker for this. The king had ultimate power, and he used this to manipulate others to get what he wanted. He even went as far as falsely accusing his wife of a crime in order to legally murder her.

One of the biggest problems with a power-over power structure is that it has us thinking we have to grab all the power that we can, as if there is a limit. It teaches us that we have to fight our way to the top and that there's not enough power for everyone. This creates a scarcity mentality. Anytime humans react—or make decisions—from a place of scarcity, we are in trouble. The truth is, there is enough power for everyone. There's enough money, resources, love, attention, and connection too. After all, power isn't pie! There's always more.

What if I was to tell you that the power-over dynamic is only one way to relate to power? There are many types of power. Power shifts, changes, and transforms. The type of power that serves in one situation may be problematic in another. As a witch, it is important to understand the different power structures and when to use each one. Being in *your* power doesn't mean always running the meeting, being in control, or being the boss. Again, that's programming from our overculture.

- **Power-Over:** This is the power structure that most of us are familiar with. This system is one of domination and scarcity. Motivation most often comes from fear. This structure lies to us by suggesting that power is a limited resource. It teaches that only those at the top have power and you must fight your way up the "ladder" to get it—and then continue to fight those behind you to keep it. In this system, everyone is your adversary.

- **Power-With:** In this structure, power is shared. It shows up in relationships and thrives in collaboration. This structure requires respect, support, and empowerment. Power-with makes it possible for differences to keep us together rather than drive us apart. We can function collectively. Power is not a resource that needs to be fought over because when we come together, we have more of it.

- **Power-Within:** This is a solo structure. Power-within has an individual realizing they inherently possess personal power, and therefore, everyone else does too. We each have capacity, we each have worth, and we can each make a difference. When we feel strong in our individual power, we can more easily accept that each person also possesses this power. It's not a competition, it is simply truth. When you have power within, it is easier to function in a power-with structure. When you have power within, it is easier to see how power-over doesn't really work.

AWAKENING AND RAISING POWER

Witches need to learn how to work with energy, which is another form of power. Sensing energy, building it up, and directing it somewhere isn't a simple task. This is a skill that often takes practice, much like most magickal and spiritual concepts.

But I'm sure you can easily think of moments in your everyday life where you have built up power or energy. When in a fight or animated conversation; when dancing, having sex, or singing; when exercising or having intense emotional reactions, especially ones that bring about uncontrollable laughter or tears ... These are all moments where power builds up.

Typically, we let the power flow through us and naturally dissipate. Think about a hysterical laughing moment. Go back to a time when you laughed so hard you couldn't stop, and every time you started to calm down, the laughter would ramp back up again. Often after a moment like this, we might feel lightheaded or disembodied. We might feel euphoric or elated. Now imagine taking that energy and directing it toward something, using that energy like a lightning rod. That's what witches do!

A witch knows how to build power, how to develop it, grow it, and channel it, all while holding a clear and grounded inner focus. Anne Boleyn might not have built her power by dancing, but she did know how to build power to utilize it when she needed it the most.

To best develop the power-building muscle, you need to reach out and feel the edges of the power your body already holds. Power is energy. It is an unseen force, and until you can run your awareness along the contours of power, it will be more challenging for you to build it up and control it.

BUILDING POWER

To practice raising power, sit in a comfortable place where you can have the soles of your feet flat on the floor. Breathe deeply and slowly. With each inhale, allow your lungs to fill as full as is comfortable. Take a pause and notice the moment between inhale and exhale. Then slowly exhale, allowing the air to exit your body with intention and awareness.

Repeat this pattern several times until you feel grounded and present.

Keep breathing and notice your connection to the earth. Imagine roots sinking down into the earth and let yourself feel that connection. Let your roots go as deep as they want to. When they reach their comfort zone, start to breathe in that earth energy, up through your roots and into your body. Continue to keep your breathing slow, intentional, and focused.

When you are ready, begin to gently rock your hips forward and back. Curl your hips a bit forward as you inhale and then push your hips backward as you exhale. Breathe in, curl your hips, and draw the earth power into your body. You can imagine it almost like sipping a really thick milkshake through a straw: It won't sink back down, but it might take a moment to fill yourself up with it.

Keep going, inhaling, curling your hips, building up that power and energy in your body until you can feel every piece of you thrumming with it. Do this for a while, at least ten minutes.

When you feel ready, slowly shift your breathing back to normal and allow your body to come to stillness. Open your eyes and look around. Feel what your body is like in the moment. You might want to slowly and carefully stand up to see what it really feels like.

Let the energy dissipate. It may take some time for the energy to release. You may want to (or need to) move your body, shake, dance, sing, go for a walk, take a shower, put your hands and feet on the earth, have an orgasm, or do something to help spend some of the energy you banked up.

Building up energy is going to take some time. Don't go into this with the expectation that you will feel something after a few breaths or a few minutes. This is about power and *ecstasis*, so devote some real time to it.

When you first try this process, just notice what it feels like to build power. How does your body react? What is it like? Also notice what you feel like afterward. Are you filled with energy and ready to tackle a project, or are you too wired? Do you need to do something to use that energy?

Then, as you go on, see how much energy you can build. Ideally, as you gain more practice, it should become easier to build up the energy and to build it more quickly.

Once you have a solid grasp of building up energy, you can take this exercise to the next level. Do this same process, but hold your wand in your hand. Before beginning, come up with a goal that you want to focus your energy toward. Is there a desire or project that could benefit from some of your focused energy? Is there a spell that you are working? As you build up the energy, focus on this goal. When your energy building reaches its apex, point your wand using your dominant hand and send the energy out of the wand and toward your goal.

The recipient of your energy could be an actual physical object, or it may be more ethereal. But either way, focus on sending that energy out in a clear and steady stream until you can feel the built-up energy waning.

When you've sent all of the energy, allow yourself to move slowly and gently. Drink plenty of water and eat something to help shift your power into a place that is more typical for you.

Write in your journal about these experiences and note your progress.

Gifts

Anne Boleyn was alluring and she knew it. There is something about being alluring that is desirable and interesting. As I write this, witchcraft is pretty alluring. Interest in witchcraft is having a bit of a revival; there is a whole witchy movement happening on social media.

What is wonderful about this movement is more people are connecting to their power, their inner witch, and mystery. Amazing! The problem with this is that it creates rhetoric where there shouldn't be. Social media can lead you to believe that witches look one way, do things one way, and follow specific rules. But witches don't, because at the root of it all, witches are rebels!

Anne Boleyn knew what her gifts were. She knew what made her special and different. In our world, we are taught that being different isn't good, and that we need to conform and fit in. But what makes you different and unique is one of the places where you can find your power.

✦ ✦ ✦ **Personal Contemplation** ✦ ✦ ✦

What are your gifts? What makes you different, unique, and maybe even a little weird? Take out your journal and write down a list of all the things that you are good at, all the things that make you special, and all the things that are your personal gifts. What are your superpowers or special skills?

This process might take you several days, so you can add more things to your list as you think of them. Remember, you don't need to write down the things you are the *best* at—just list all the things that make you special.

After a few days, write out an affirmation for yourself. It should be a short list of five to six things that you are proud of from your list. Write these things out, beginning each sentence with "I AM." Your list might look this:

I AM funny.

I AM wise.

I AM a musician.

I AM kind.

I AM a business owner.

I AM detail oriented.

Keep this list in a place where you can see it often. Read it out loud to yourself every morning.

Walking in Two Worlds

Sometimes witches have to walk in two worlds. Not everyone lives a life that allows them to be out of the broom closet. If Anne Boleyn had been charged with witchcraft, it would have carried a life sentence. There are people all over the world being persecuted for witchcraft. Often, these people are not even witches—much like the witch trials of Salem and Europe. But there are places where it is still dangerous to call yourself a witch.

If Anne Boleyn was practicing witchcraft, it would have to have been done in silence and secret. This is what it is to walk in two worlds. In my fantasy story of Anne actually practicing witchcraft, there is Anne the Queen and then there is Anne the Witch, keeping her magick hidden in the shadows. Those two identities would have been kept apart, one hidden from the public the other lives in.

And for many modern-day witches, this is still the case. Many witches I know have one social media presence for their family and work colleagues and another for their spiritual pursuits. Being out of the broom closet doesn't make you a better witch or a more spiritually capable person.

Walking between two worlds is a very real part of witchcraft. You have to get good at code switching, changing the way that you speak or respond while in different company. You have to master the art of "keeping silent." But the world shouldn't be this way. We should all be free to be who we are no matter the situation we are in. We can do the work to change the world, but we also must survive in it. Don't feel ashamed for having to walk in two worlds.

⟨ Traveling to the Realm of Anne Boleyn ⟩

We don't have to time travel back to the 1500s, wear courtly finery, and have lessons in flirting to connect with the power of Anne Boleyn. If you are having trouble finding your own power in daunting circumstances or if you are hiding who you are from people you care about, connecting with Anne Boleyn may help you find answers and the best way forward.

Supplies: An image of Anne Boleyn, frankincense incense, incense burner, glass of wine or grape juice, and a vase of flowers.

Set Up: Take all of the supplies and create a small altar. Start with the image of Anne in the center and build around it. Light the frankincense incense and keep it burning. Pour the wine or grape juice for Anne. Knock three times on the surface of your altar and say her name out loud.

Sit or lie down. Let yourself be as comfortable as possible. Begin the trance.

Trance: Lie down or sit comfortably. Allow yourself to gently relax while taking some slow and easy breaths. As you breathe, allow the edges of your body to soften. With each breath, the space between your cells grows larger and larger. Allow yourself to feel as if you are gently floating.

From this place of expansion, allow your witch's eye to open. Your witch's eye is the eye that sits above and between your normal seeing eyes. Open the eye up and see before you a downward-spiraling staircase. The walls are made of thick stone bricks with torches in sconces every few feet along the wall.

Take a step down the stairs and then another. Continue to walk down, down, down the spiraling stone staircase. One step at a time, you move ever further downward, the torches gently lighting the stairway. (Pause.)

One foot in front of the other, you continue to move down, down, down. (Pause.)

As you reach the bottom of the staircase, you see before you a large door. Take a moment to explore this door. What is it made from? Are there any designs or decorations on it? What does the door handle look like? Take a moment to notice the intricacies of this door. (Pause.)

On the other side of this door is Anne Boleyn's waiting room. Say her name, knock three times, and turn the handle.

Step inside the waiting room of Anne Boleyn. She is there with an herbal tea service set, calmly waiting for you. She pours out a cup of tea for you, gesturing for you to come in and sit. You can smell the scent of your favorite tea. Approach her, offer a bow, and speak with this queen. Ask her about your own gifts and power. (Long pause.)

Remember that your time in this realm is limited. If there are any questions in your heart that you long to ask, ask them now. (Long pause.)

For now, you must leave this realm. Offer your thanks and gratitude to Anne Boleyn, knowing that you can return to this place any time you need. (Pause.)

When you are ready, turn and step through the door that brought you into her chambers. The door closes softly behind you as you return to the bottom of the spiraling staircase. Begin the ascent back up the stairs.

With one foot in front of the other, you move up the spiraling staircase. Follow along the stone stairs with the softly glowing torches guiding your way. Step by step, you move back up, up, up, coming back to your own space.

You take one step at a time until you reach the top of the stairs. From there, close your witch's eye, that all-knowing eye, allowing it to return to its normal state.

Notice what it is to be in your body now. Breathe, allowing the inhale and exhale to firm up your edges. Breathe and let yourself fully integrate with your body. Notice your edges and what it is like to be you in this moment. Tap the edges of your body, allowing yourself to be fully present in the room. When you feel ready, slowly and gently open your eyes. Place your hands on the top of your head and say your name three times out loud.

Welcome back!

Take the flowers and drink outside and leave them near a tree or plant, if possible. Speak your gratitude to Anne Boleyn out loud and thank her for your experience with her.

Being a Witch with Anne Boleyn

The path of the witch with Anne Boleyn as your guide is one that will always keep you on your toes. This is the path of power. How can you use your gifts and skills to help fuel your success in the world?

Anne knew what made her special and unique, and she wore those things like a badge of honor. She was smart, proud, and independent. These were her gifts.

We witches need to know our own personal gifts. These are skills we are just naturally good at, abilities we have spent years learning, and things that make us unique. We witches need to celebrate ourselves. Again, this is the path of knowing thyself.

Love what makes you special and different. Love what you have worked hard to achieve.

Anne Boleyn used her skills and uniqueness to gain power. We can learn from her. How do we develop our power of self? How do we stand up and work for a power-with structure? How do we dismantle structures of power-over?

✦ ✦ ✦ Witch Contemplation ✦ ✦ ✦

Where in your life can you see yourself embodying power and independence like Anne Boleyn? Take out your journal and free write on the topic of power. How does this concept make you feel? How does this word make you feel? Set a timer and give yourself fifteen minutes to write whatever comes up.

At the end of the timer, go back and circle five words that stand out as charged—either positively or negatively. Then write a prayer, poem, or affirmation for healthy power in your life using these five words.

CHAPTER 7

MARIE LAVEAU

Marie Laveau is probably the most famous witch of the United States. She was a woman of color whose grandmother was enslaved. Marie was born and raised in New Orleans, during a difficult historical time in the South, both because of racist laws around slavery, segregation, and oppression but also because of serious disease outbreaks. It was a dangerous time and yet, Marie thrived.

The most interesting thing about Marie Laveau is that her legends live on. These legends are not just from the facts we know about her; they come from rumors, whispers, and the fascinating mythology of her life. There is so much speculation about her. Even the years of her birth (likely 1798) and death (likely 1881) are uncertain.

As a devout Christian and Voudou priestess, Marie probably would not have called herself a witch, but we know she did practice magick, rituals, and spells. Of course, I'm using these words from the modern perspective I have. Her faith was her own. Those that practice Voudou, even in modern times, don't typically call what they do witchcraft because Voudou is a religion in and of itself.

I'm using the spelling *Voudou* because that is how it is spelled in the book *A New Orleans Voudou Priestess*, which was one of my main reference books in learning about Mama Marie. You will also see this word spelled Voodoo, Voudon, Voudou, Voo-Doo, and many other ways. These differences in spelling seem to be regional and dialect based.

As we move forward inspired by the power and heretical nature of Marie Laveau, I want to be clear and transparent about something: This section is not about Voudou or how to practice in that religious system. Voudou is an initiatory religion. To fully participate and understand how that tradition works, you need to be a part of that spiritual community. If you are interested in getting involved with Voudou, seek out a Voudou house to train you in that lineage.

Voudou is an initiatory religious system; you don't just jump into it. It requires training, initiation, and community connection. One of the ways Marie connected her Voudou training to her community was through the rituals that she would lead on the shores of Lake Pontchartrain. Spirituality and devotion were very important to Marie. On top of Voudou rituals and spiritual workings, she would also attend church every Sunday and had a strong relationship with several deities.

Marie received her Voudou training either from her mother and grandmother or from a former Voudou Queen of New Orleans; we don't actually know. But what is important is the lineage was handed down from woman to woman. And we know that

Marie passed the tradition on to her own children and descendants—most famously her daughter, who became known as Marie the II. Marie had nine children, two with her first husband and the rest with her second. Marie outlived both of her husbands and had a nickname of the Widow Paris, Paris being the surname of her first husband.

Marie was referred to as the "Voudou Queen of New Orleans," and we know from historical accounts it was likely sometime in the 1820s that Marie started to make a public name for herself in relationship to Voudou. By the 1850s Marie often found her name mentioned in the local newspapers, where there were all sorts of wild stories written about her; the validity of these articles is highly suspect. Some of the stories are far more interesting than the likely reality, but that is part of her magick.

There are many stories about Marie that cannot be proven or disproven. But there is an undercurrent of belief in them, whether they were the truth or not. Ultimately, their truth doesn't matter because enough folks believe them to be true. They have become a part of Marie's lineage, mystery, and magick.

Here are some common stories that are potentially true about Marie.

- She was known to visit men on death row, helping them build altars in their cells and pray for forgiveness or for the truth to be seen. Some stories survive of Marie feeding poisoned gumbo to death row inmates the night before they were going to face the gallows.

- Marie was known to take care of those who were severely ill. During her time, New Orleans was overrun with several serious illnesses like smallpox, malaria, yellow fever, and cholera. Marie would minister to those suffering, putting herself in danger.

- Tales are told of Marie opening her home to women on the run from abusive situations. One of these tales tells of a Native American woman and her children who lived in a small dwelling in Marie's backyard for many years.

- Marie may have offered hairdressing services, which would have put her in front of a lot of people with access to wealthy folks' homes. It was through these relationships that Marie was able to learn the secrets of wealthy and powerful New Orleanians. It is believed she would use these secrets to blackmail powerful people, both for money and for favors.

When we find a woman like Marie, remembered by people all over the world as a powerful witch, it tells me that there has to be some truth in those stories. There was no social media, no Instagram, no Twitter, where Marie could paint the image of being a powerful practitioner. No, she had to walk the talk—remember integrity? What is known about her is mainly from word of mouth, from stories handed down, and from newspaper stories written about her. Rumor may not be more powerful than truth, but it sure does last longer.

If we look at this powerful witch based on her legend, it's akin to elevating an ancestor. She takes on mythic proportions. She becomes a sign, symbol, and beacon for those who hear her name and learn her story. What is remembered lives, and how one is remembered is just as important to the ancestor as what they did in life. A witch ancestor she is!

The legends of this (in)famous witch are likely larger than the reality, but that is also part of the power of Marie Laveau. She has lived on in the minds of those who know of American witchcraft. Her power has grown, so much so that there is a temple in her name in New Orleans and she is considered the patron saint of the city.

OF ALTARS AND COMMUNITY

Community is one of the most important relationships we have. Community can look a million different ways: family, friends, coworkers, spiritual groups, etc. Being connected to a community, in whatever fashion that may look like, keeps us accountable. Marie Laveau shows us how to serve the community in order to help the people in our lives thrive and improve.

This may surprise you, but being involved with and connected to communities is a big part of being a heretic. It does the world no good to stay alone, apart, and disconnected. No matter how it looks, we really do need community. It is what supports us, helps us, guides us, and occasionally calls us out on our bullshit.

In the legends about Marie Laveau, altars loom large. Descriptions of the altars in her home and at the rituals she presided over are part of many personal accounts: "Frequent visitors to the Laveau-Glapion home talked of rooms filled with altars, candles, and images of the saints, a fact also mentioned in the Picayune's Guide to New Orleans for 1887 and 1900."[9]

---

9. Long, *New Orleans Voudou Priestess*, 108.

In a way, altars become the focal point of spiritual life. An altar or shrine connects us to mystery and magick. Altars serve as a portal, an opening, between who we are, where we are, and where and who we want to be.

Altars

Altars and shrines are a big part of the Marie Laveau legacy. Stories and descriptions of the altars she would build are in many, if not most, of the stories told about her in written records: "Her altar was in the last room of the house on St. Anne Street. I'm positive she had no saints on that altar. It took the width of the room, and had large plaster statues of a bear, a lion, and a tiger, paper flowers, and candles."[10] And the altars at the rituals she led at the lakeside are legendary; they included food, drinks, taxidermized animals, snakes, candles, and drumming.

Her magick in connection to altars has led to altars being created in her honor. In some ways, the spirit of Marie has been kept alive by the altars that exist for her. Of course, many of these altars are in New Orleans. One of the most famous is the shrine at the New Orleans Healing Center that is maintained by Sallie Ann Glassman. This altar is visited by people from all over the world who want to pay homage to the Voudou Queen of New Orleans.

CREATING AN ALTAR

One of the most common questions I get asked is "How do I create an altar?" Depending on your proclivities, the answer to the question will either make you divinely happy or super frustrated. The truth is, there isn't one correct way to create an altar. So, I

---

10. Morrow Long, *New Orleans Voudou Priestess*, 110.

must ask in return, "How do you *want* to create an altar?" Unless you are training in a specific tradition or lineage, an altar can look like whatever you want or need it to.

Altars can be created for any purpose. Here are just a few examples of altars:

- **Ancestor Shrine:** An ancestral shrine is a place reserved for your ancestors. This altar may contain images of ancestors; fabrics from different countries; offerings of food, drink, flowers, incense, or other specific items; and candles, ashes, bones, skulls, or other trinkets that are uniquely special to you, your beloved dead, and your ancestral lineage.

- **Working Altar:** A working altar is a place where you do your spiritual work. You may choose to use this altar to pray, meditate, sing, burn offerings, do your spell workings, or do a myriad of other spiritual works.

- **Devotional Shrine:** A devotional shrine is typically dedicated to a specific deity or spiritual ally. These altars may contain statues of the deity, offerings for the deity, and other decorations that would appeal to the deity the altar was created for.

- **Spell Altar:** Spell altars are often temporary spaces. You set up your spell altar, work your spell, and then clean the altar up. The altar exists only as long as it needs to in order to complete the working.

- **Seasonal Altar:** Seasonal altars hold decorations for the changing of the seasons. You may want to follow the Pagan Wheel of the Year or, better yet, create seasonal altars for where you live. For example, in September and October in Northern California, we have "the crush," which is the time of year when the grapes are harvested. Setting up a seasonal altar with grapes and wine would honor that seasonal change.

An altar can be as simple as a candle and a glass of water or as elaborate as a room full of treasures and trinkets.

✦ ✦ ✦ Is It a Shrine or an Altar? ✦ ✦ ✦

Yes! Why not both? An altar is a general descriptive term for any place set aside for devotion, magick, or prayer, while a shrine is more specifically a place of devotion. Shrines are for ancestors, deities, or other spiritual allies. A shrine falls under the umbrella term of an altar. However, an altar might not be a shrine.

Got it?

Community

One thing is for sure, Marie Laveau served her community. We see this in the stories of her leading rituals, taking care of the ill, and ministering to those sentenced to death. She looked out for those that had no one else, including women on the run.

This is an important part of her story and energy. Witches, heretics, and warrior women all need to find their clan. Having community gives you a place to find support and understanding. Community is a place that keeps you on track and calls you on your bullshit, and being in service to a community can be very rewarding. Acts of services are a big part of many spiritual traditions, which we'll explore more in a moment.

It's not uncommon to see witches push back against the concept of community. There are lots of reasons for this. For some, in-person community isn't possible; there may not be enough local, like-minded people to form a collective clan of folks to connect with. For others, community dynamics and complicated interpersonal relationships can make being involved with community a challenge.

Any time there is a discussion about the challenges of community, there are always folks who make comments like "That's why I'm a solitary." Yeah, I get it, being on your own is rewarding and wonderful. Being able to call your own shots, make your own decisions, and do things exactly how you want to is powerful. *But* we all need to connect with other people.

Humans need other humans. And it's so much more rewarding if we have commonality in belief with those other humans.

There's a long-standing joke that's told in the Reclaiming tradition of witchcraft circles, and in many other places too. It goes something like this: "The best thing about community is all the people, and the worst thing about community is all the people."

Here's the thing about being a witch and connecting to community. When you do spiritual work, you grow and evolve as a person. When you do work with community, it's like taking a quantum leap in your spiritual work. Exploring your spiritual side on your own will only get you so far. You need other people to show you different ways, thoughts, approaches, and ideas. You can't—literally can't—find all of the answers on your own. Real, dramatic growth happens in the arms of community.

Community can look a lot of different ways. You might want to be in a coven, start a coven or learning circle, join a public ritual planning group, sign up for classes, join an online witch community, or start an online forum for witchcraft discussion. It doesn't matter *how* you connect to your clan, but it is important that you *do* connect to your clan.

And this brings us back to the idea of service. We all need to serve our communities, whether that is in our coven, witch clans, or other mundane communities. Abundance is based on the cyclic nature of the world. To receive, you gotta give. So how are you giving back to community?

ACTS OF SERVICE

All religions have a concept around acts of service. It's great when you can tithe or donate money to the cause, but it is also important to put your skin in the game. This goes beyond the idea of volunteering, although volunteering is an accurate description. Acts of service are done with the intention of giving yourself to community. Very simply, acts of service are performing a task to take the burden off someone else.

There is a selfish undercurrent in witchcraft because so much of it is focused on getting what you want and working to improve your own personal circumstances. But your personal witchcraft is just part of a bigger picture. I believe we need to implement acts of service into our communities as something we do with conscious awareness. It needs to be a part of clan conversations. How are we giving back? How are we taking care of each other?

Witches and heretics know that we don't live in a bubble. We don't exist on an island. We need to nurture our relationships with the land we live on, the people that live with us, and the members of our community.

✦ ✦ ✦ Ways to Serve Your Community ✦ ✦ ✦

Meet your neighbors. Your neighbors might not be cool with you wearing your black witch's hat over for dinner, but your neighborhood is a great place to start connecting to community. Learn your neighbor's names. Keep an eye out for each other. You don't have to be best friends, but you can at least be acquaintances.

Perform random acts of beauty. Guerilla acts of beauty are one of my favorite things in the world. (If you'd like to learn more about the concept of guerilla acts of beauty, check out my book *Walking in Beauty*.) Small acts of kindness help you to connect to your clan by spreading joy and beauty where you live. Pay for the person behind you at the drive-through, leave a sweet note on a random car's windshield, or place a sticky note with an uplifting message on the mirror in a public bathroom. Spread beauty in your location.

Donate your time. Sign up for a soup kitchen or food bank. Spend some time serving others in need. Sign up for a service that builds houses for the homeless, offer your sweat equity for a local school, or offer to work a few hours a week at the local animal shelter.

Pick up trash. Join a local movement to clean up a park or beach. If there aren't any events happening, start one. Or just take a trash bag with you to a local green space and spend a few hours cleaning up.

Donate money. Nonprofits are constantly looking for financial help. Find a nonprofit that services your community in a way that is meaningful to you and donate.

LEVELING UP YOUR CLAN

As you step more into your rebel self and fully awaken your witchy nature, you might notice the people around you feeling uncomfortable. As you grow and change, you might start to outgrow the relationship in your life. You will start to notice what is no longer working. You will start to set boundaries and make it clear what is and is not acceptable in your life.

If you want to be a rebel, you might have to cut off relationships that are harmful, abusive, or wrong for you. As you embrace your witch self, you might get pushback from friends and loved ones. They might start to see the changes you are going through and not like it. This is typically because there is fear; they see you growing and don't want you to leave them behind.

And yet, sometimes leaving them behind is your only option.

As you connect to community, you are going to find your rebel kin. These are the people who will support your growth and changes. These are the folks who want you to succeed. These are the kin who will share what they have learned to help you along your path. You need to surround yourself with people who match the vibration for where you want to go in life.

Letting go of problematic relationships is a hard but necessary part of becoming the rebel. The process of clearing out the connections that no longer serve you can hurt, but you will be better for it in the long run.

WALKING IN THIS WORLD

A big part of Voudou is working with saints. None of what we are about to discuss is initiatory Voudou information; saints are honored and revered in many spiritual systems. One saint has become connected with Marie Laveau because it seems she took special interest in honoring their feast day. That saint is Saint John the Baptist. There are many Voudou lineages that honor St. John on St. John's Eve, June 23, which falls very close to the Summer Solstice. Stories of what would happen at a St. John's Eve celebration would range from drumming and dancing to full-on orgies.

For years all the major newspapers in New Orleans would write about the events at a St. John's Eve celebration. The event became a popular tourist draw. Thousands of people would flock to the city to see the Voudou Queen of New Orleans leading a ritual. More often than not, people were left disappointed because no one practicing Voudou would actually show up.

It's believed by many that Marie did hold rituals on St. John's Eve, but these were small, private, and hidden, while public announcements were intentionally made to lead the looky-loos to the wrong places. The small amount of detail that does seem to be true paints a story of joyous celebration. There are many "eye witness" accounts of St. John's Eve events taking place with folks gathering and sharing food, drumming, and singing together.

Whether you work with saints in your personal practice or not, there is a way to add feast days, holy days, and private celebrations into your personal spiritual calendar. Spiritual traditions don't have to be dictated by outside sources. Take out a yearly calendar and find dates that are important to you and your family or community. These could be birthdays, anniversaries, death dates, coven start dates, specific deity feast days, or other special moments. For example, when my daughter was a little kid, she made up Disco Night, which is on March 18. We dress up and play disco music and dance around the house. It's become a feast day celebration for our family.

More recently, a seven-year-old in New Zealand received international attention when his home-created holiday called Wolfenoot went viral.[11] It's simply a holiday where people who have been kind to dogs are visited by the wolf spirit and left gifts. Sounds pretty good to me. It's celebrated on November 23, so mark that one down in your calendars if you've been good to dogs this year.

What are special days or holidays that are unique to your family or clan? Can you turn them into feast days and take a moment to honor what is special about your life and your loved ones? The more reasons and opportunities we have the celebrate, the better!

◎ Traveling to the Realm of Marie Laveau ◎

A big part of the spiritual practice that Marie Laveau was involved with included drumming and dance. Trance states can come in a myriad of ways. Many of us think of meditation or trance as a practice that happens when we relax, perhaps lying down, and go on an imaginary journey.

However, there are many traditions where the journey happens through the physical exhaustion of the body. Spending hours listening to a drum rhythm and moving your body can lead to ecstatic out-of-body experiences. These practices are seen in many of the Voudou rituals that Marie would have led and participated in.

As Voudou is an initiatory tradition, I do not recommend taking on a ritual in this tradition without proper guidance and training. We can visit with Marie in a trance without a physically ecstatic process. However, if you find yourself feeling connected

---

11. NZ Herald, "Kiwi Boy, 7, Invents Wolf Holiday and It Has Already Gone Viral."

to her and want to seek out deeper training in Voudou, search for teachers in that lineage to learn more.

Supplies: An image of Marie Laveau, a purple glass-encased candle, and holy water (or water that has been spiritually blessed).

Set Up: You will want to create a small altar. To begin, sprinkle the area with holy water and then place the image of Marie Laveau in the center of the space. Place the remaining holy water next to the image with the purple candle.

Light the purple candle and say:

Mama Marie, Mama Marie, Mama Marie
I call to you, Queen of New Orleans
Guide me on my journey
Show me the way
Hear my prayers
And visit with me this day

Lie down or get comfortable and begin the trance.

Trance: Get comfortable and focus on your breathing. Allow the air to flow in and out as normally and comfortably as possible. Let your focus just follow along without trying to force your breathing. Notice how easy and simple this act of following your breath is. (Pause.)

Let yourself slowly sink down wherever you are. Connect to your current physical location and allow yourself to sink. This process is slow and easy and safe. Your breath continues to flow in and out with ease. All the while, you continue to go deeper and deeper and deeper, connecting into the water table that flows right below the surface of the earth.

As you connect with that primal water source, your inner witch's eye opens and you take in the wonder of the living water table: the caves, the structures, the flow, the power of this water. You connect more deeply, carried by the gentle ebb and flow of the water. You are held and safe. As you relax, the water below the earth begins to carry you gently along, and you can feel the tides and currents move you forward. Flowing, flowing, flowing. (Pause.)

You notice a shift in the water, a rising and a soft pulling. The water lifts you up and out onto the shores of Lake Pontchartrain. As you rise out of the waters, warm and dry, Marie Laveau stands before you. You can hear the soft lapping of the lake against the shoreline and a steady, rhythmic drumbeat. Behind Marie is a group of revelers playing instruments and singing. You can feel the music move through your body. It feels like a thrumming that matches your heartbeat. (Pause.)

Marie begins to slowly sway back and forth in front of you and you find yourself moving along, matching her movements. She says something to you in Creole, and you know exactly what it means.

Take a moment to speak with the Voudou Queen of New Orleans. Ask her your questions about witchcraft and community and see what wisdom she holds for you. (Long pause.)

Marie walks you back to the edge of the lake and dips her fingers into the water. She anoints your brow, and you feel the blessing sink into your skin. (Pause.)

Remember that although you can return to the shores of this lake at any time, for now your time in this realm is limited. Say any last words that are in your heart and remember to offer your gratitude to Marie Laveau. (Long pause.)

When you are ready, Marie gestures for you to return to the water. She helps you lie down and offers you a second blessing, sprinkling the waters of the lake across your forehead. You are held by the waters of Lake Pontchartrain, safe and secure. Breathe and relax and feel how you are carried along by the water, gently and safely. Flowing, flowing, flowing.

As you float away, the water begins to join forces with all of the waters of the world, and you continue to be carried and buoyed by the water. You feel your witch's eye beginning to close, returning to its normal state of being. (Pause.)

Again, you feel yourself rising from the depths of the water, lifting ever upward and back into the familiar comforts of your human body. Feel the edges of your body begin to firm, returning to normal and welcoming you home. Notice your breathing, the easy inhale and exhale. Let yourself become firm, solid, and whole. (Pause.)

When you feel ready, slowly tap your edges, using the palm of your hands against your skin. Place your hands on the top of your head and open your eyes. Look around the room you are in, taking note of anything that catches your eye. Say your name out loud three times.

Welcome back!

Blow out the candle and say thank you to Marie Laveau for her support throughout your journey. Take time to write down anything interesting or important about your experience.

Being a Witch with Marie Laveau

Marie Laveau shows us how to not only be a witch in charge, but how to use our power to help other people. What good is the practice of magick if we don't do anything with it? All rebels are brave, but witches must be doubly so. Marie Laveau can help you to be bold and hone your witchcraft to a razor-sharp point, even if you must remain in the broom closet.

The Voudou Queen of New Orleans can help you step fully into yourself. She can help you find your boldness and be unequivocally you. There are lots of rumors about the life and times of Marie, and we will never really know the full truth. It's not farfetched to think these rumors were also known to Marie—she may have even benefited from them.

Because she survived the very public rumor mill and made it work to her benefit, this is another place Marie can strengthen your power as a witch. How can you walk with your head held high and not worry about what "they" say or what "they" think about you? How can you take the rumors and make them work on your behalf?

Marie Laveau is a witch of community. She took the time to have her private practice, but she also took the time to do her work for the world. We know that she was a deeply spiritual woman, but she didn't hoard her spiritual life like a dragon. She shared her knowledge and experience. She helped those in need. Marie Laveau was a perfect example of walking your talk.

Remember, community looks a lot of different ways. As we grow out of childhood, we have the amazing opportunity to pick our people. Our people, our clan, may be family members, community members, coven members, work mates, school mates, collected friends, or online folks. The importance of community is not who the members of the community are, but rather the connections that are made.

This is the power of Marie Laveau.

✦ ✦ ✦ Witch Contemplation ✦ ✦ ✦

Where in your life do you see yourself in connection and community like Marie Laveau? How do you feel about community and your relationships with others in community? Write down your ultimate desire for community. What would your ideal community look like, act like, and be like?

Let yourself look deeper. Have you felt this in a group before? Do you feel this in any groups now? What would it take to find people to fulfill this desire?

Write down five steps you could take to begin building this ideal community for yourself. Go and take one of these steps now.

PART THREE

BEING THE HERETIC

CHAPTER 8
THE HERETICS

What reaction do you have to the word *heretic*? Does the word describe a "bad" person? Is a heretic someone you would want to avoid? Is it a title that you never want to be associated with? By dictionary definition, a heretic is someone practicing religious heresy. Heresy is the belief of something outside the established customs of a religious organization. For the purposes of this book, let's take that one step further: Heresy is the belief of something outside of *culturally established customs*. Heretical people look at the status quo and think, *Nah, I don't want anything to do with that.* Heretics want to do things their own way and buck restrictions, forced trends, or cultural norms. Heretics are willing to give a big middle finger to conforming.

Owning the title of heretic is a recent revelation for me personally. It all started when something I had said on social media was called heretical. This feedback was offered as a compliment, and I took it as one. I don't want to go with the grain, especially when that grain is the cause of systemic racism, oppression, transphobia, and puritanical repression.

To own the honor of being a heretic is an even bolder step than taking on the title of witch. Heretics often became martyrs. Heretics put themselves on the line and become symbols of change. The times we are currently living in—as I sit writing these words—is a time when humanity is facing the potential of global upheaval and traumatic change. Many of us feel like the capitalist system we are all so used to is beginning to crumble. We are experiencing the death throes of patriarchy. And it's not going away quietly or easily.

I hoped it would simply exit stage right, but patriarchy is fighting for every moment it has left of its life. It would be easy to give in and go back to accepting the status quo. But we can't do that. We must keep going, pushing forward, and finding more heretics to help shift these changes more quickly.

This is why we need you, heretic! Heretics are the ones that hold the tide of transformation. They are both the death and birth midwives, understanding the end of one thing is the beginning of another. The heretic is the one with the sword, ending the life of the patriarchy (remember Éowyn from *The Lord of the Rings*?), but the heretic is also the one laboring to bring the new paradigm into being. Declaring yourself a witch is a personal title, an individual acceptance of who you are; declaring yourself a heretic takes on another level of intensity. It's no longer a secret you can keep.

A heretic must take action on their beliefs. They must be at the forefront to lead the revolution. The job of the heretic is an important one to the survival of witches and warriors across the planet. Indeed, their role is imperative to the survival of the planet itself.

Are you feeling the call of the wild? Are you feeling the blood stirring within you, beseeching you to take a stand? Are you ready to be a heretic or to finally admit to the world that you are one? Come on, friend, let's take the leap together. Here's my hand. Let's do this!

THE CAULDRON

The tool of the heretic is the cauldron. The cauldron is a tool of transformation. You put something into it, apply some form of alchemy, and voilà! You end up with something else. Magick! Transformation! Not to mention the hundreds of stories from all over the world where cauldrons are used to make potions, hold never-ending drink, bring soldiers back from the dead, and many other magickal feats. Sure, cauldrons have a practical purpose (they're for cooking food), but they have taken on a magickal and mysterious flair thanks to folklore about witches.

This is why the cauldron is the perfect tool for the heretic. A tool that is seemingly mundane actually holds an immense amount of mystery. Don't judge it by its simple look. There's a lot of power in that simple bowl.

A cauldron is a place of transformation—you might even go so far as to think of the cauldron as *the* tool of alchemy. And truly, all the alchemists were heretics.

You can get cauldrons at your local metaphysical shop, at thrift or vintage shops, or even cooking supply shops. A traditional cauldron is made from cast iron, but you can use any fire-safe container as a cauldron. Make sure whatever you use is fire-safe, otherwise your container could melt or explode. Keep your cauldron on a heat-resistant surface.

☙ Cauldron of Transformation ❧

Complete this ritual when you are ready to let go of personal limiting beliefs and to step into being your full heretical self. Take some time ahead of this ritual to meditate or journal on a limiting belief that is keeping you from achieving your goals. Then be honest with yourself: What is stopping you from taking your first step toward a power-full life? Is it fear? Is it imposter syndrome? See if you can narrow your blockage down to a single word or short phrase. Remember, we are working with *one* limiting belief—not all of them.

This ritual is best performed on a new moon, outdoors if possible.

Supplies: A firesafe container (cauldron), a piece of paper and a pen, incense like dragon's blood or frankincense, a glass-encased white candle, and a cup of water.

Set Up: Place your firesafe container in the center of your ritual space. Have all the other items close at hand. Set them up in a way that is pleasing to you.

Light the incense and the candle. Give yourself some time to contemplate what limiting belief you are ready to let go of. You may want to read over any journal notes that you wrote to prepare you for this.

When you've come up with your word or phrase, write it down on the piece of paper. Say the word or phrase out loud. Then say, "I release you."

Light the paper on fire and place it in the cauldron. Watch as it burns and make sure it burns completely. When the paper has finished burning, pick up the incense and trace the smoke around your body as a smoke cleanse.

Contemplate, meditate, or journal on what you want to call in. This might be the opposite word of what you've just released, or it may be something else.

When you are ready, use the pointer finger of your dominant hand to write your new word on the surface of the water in the cup. Say the new word out loud. Then say, "I take you in."

Drink the full cup of water. Repeat this ritual any time you discover another limiting belief that you want to release.

✦ ✦ ✦ Personal Contemplation ✦ ✦ ✦

Do you feel like a heretic? Do you already see places in your life where you live outside of the mainstream? How do you imagine being a heretic would change your life?

Take out your journal and write the word HERETIC across the top of the page. Set a timer for five minutes and free write on this word. Anything and everything that comes up is fair game.

When the timer goes off, set your journal aside for at least one full day. When you feel ready, read over what you've written. How does it make you feel?

Then write the words I AM A HERETIC on the top of a new page. Set a time for five minutes and free write on what comes up for you with this statement.

When the timer goes off, set your journal aside for at least one full day. When you are ready, read over what you've written. How does all of this make you feel? Are you ready to call yourself a heretic?

HERETICS OF THIS BOOK

You may notice all the heretics in this section have something in common. They are deeply religious women. Because of their love and devotion to the truth of their faith, they turned against the status quo and put themselves in grave danger. They fought against the tides of the patriarchy and stood up when it was perilously dangerous to do so.

Yes, these women are religious, but you don't have to be of any specific faith to feel the heretical blood in your veins. Heretics come in all spiritual forms.

In the following chapters, we will explore three famous women: Mary Magdalene, Jeanne D'Arc (Joan of Arc), and Salome. You will have a chance to learn more about them, connect with their powers, and take one more step on your path to being a heretic.

With that, let's be on our way…

CHAPTER 9
MARY MAGDALENE

There is so much speculation about Mary Magdalene, and there are many voracious modern people who are worshippers of this historical woman. She has taken on a cultlike following. As I've mentioned before, I wasn't raised in a religious home. I did not have a deep childhood relationship with Mary Magdalene like many folks do, which means what I am sharing here comes from what I have personally learned and studied on my own in the last few years.

I don't know which stories about Mary Magdalene are true, which ones are twisted (even delightfully so), and which ones are outright lies. And let's be honest, we will never know which stories about her are true. That's an important thing to remember: Which stories are true and which are not isn't the point. None of that matters. Yes, we should learn the history and read historical records when we can, but modern egregore holds a lot of power. And let me tell you, Mary Magdalene's modern egregore is powerful.

First, it is important to know Mary Magdalene's name was not Mary Magdalene. In fact, she was from the village of Magdala or

Magdalene. Jesus hung out with a lot of Marys (it was a very popular woman's name), and this has caused a lot of speculation and debate about which of the Marys is *the* Mary. Some believe that Magdalene is a title, like Priestess, and there are those who believe she was a priestess of Ashtaroth or one of the other ancient Jewish goddesses. This is why, in some retellings, her name is Mary the Magdalene or Mary of Magdala. But for simplicity's sake, I will refer to her as Mary Magdalene.

In one version of the story, Mary Magdalene was a prostitute who gave up her work to travel with Jesus and his followers and through this, she ended up being one of his disciples. In another version of the story, she was the wife of Jesus and taught lessons of love and community by his side. Sex worker, wife, or both, we don't really know. I believe the most important facet of these stories is the one consistent piece: Mary Magdalene was a disciple of Jesus. She was one of his close companions. She traveled with him and the other disciples, teaching the gospel of love and understanding and performing miracles and healings.

Yes, Jesus was the one performing the bulk of the miracles, healings, and magick, but all his followers did the good work too. It was rare for a woman to travel in the desert, teaching about love and connection with God along with a group of rebellious men.

Mary Magdalene was indeed a rare woman.

In her time, she lived in a hotbed of civil unrest. There were complicated and dangerous political factions, all vying for control. Most of these systems were built on traditions of patriarchy, where women had very little power or even autonomy.

Mary Magdalene believed in the power of love and the message of connection. She traveled with thirteen men as they spoke truth to power. Their lives would have been simple, and the more attention and followers they gained, the more they would have been in danger simply for going against the status quo. But she so deeply believed in the messages and the changes their part of the world needed that she put her life on the line every single day.

Married to Jesus or not, witnessing his death would have been highly traumatic to say the least. And sadly, if she was his wife, she would not have been safe after his death. She would have become the next target for "the powers that be" as well as some of Jesus's own followers. She could have potentially been accused of the same crimes as Jesus. And if she was truly with child, as some stories proclaim, there would have been plenty of factions who would not want her child to live.

All of that is quite a lot for one woman to bear on her own.

There are stories of Mary Magdalene running away from the Middle East after her beloved was killed, pregnant with his child. There are stories of her coming ashore in France, where a holy order was formed. And in the basement of the basilica in the town of Saint-Maximin-la-Sainte-Baume, there is a relic that many believe to be the skull of Mary Magdalene.[12]

The legends talk of a cave not far from that small French town where there is a hidden monastery. It is at this place that legend says Mary Magdalene lived after arriving in France. She lived alone in a cave, started her own sisterhood, and was revered by the locals as a wise woman.

There are also groups of women who have accepted Mary Magdalene, also referred to as *The Magdalene*, as an entity of higher spiritual evolution. There are groups who offer "rose channel activations" that were channeled from the spiritual essence of Mary Magdalene to help women step more deeply into their personal power and increase their spiritual awareness.

---

12. Samantha, "The Skull and Bones of Mary Magdalane."

I can't speak to the validity of any of this, but there are thousands of people all over the globe who pay homage to Mary Magdalene as a spirit beyond the teachings of Jesus and his followers. And I'll tell you what, modern egregore holds a lot of water. The more people believe in something, the stronger that something becomes.

There are enough modern lovers of The Magdalene. There are plenty of people who follow her, pray to her, pay homage to her, and believe she is the emissary of divine love. The power of those beliefs has made Mary Magdalene stronger. Her rosy light touches something deep in modern people, especially women. She can show us the way to love and heart healing.

I don't know about you, but I think the world could use a lot of love and heart healing.

One magickal tenant that comes not from Mary Magdalene but from Aleister Crowley is "Love is the law, love under will."[13] Although I highly doubt Aleister Crowley was a devotee of Mary Magdalene, his feelings around love being the law are very much in alignment with the energy of The Magdalene.

When taken out of original context, the phrase "love is the law" creates an impression that if only we have love, life will be easy, simple, sweet, and twee. Love your enemy, and all that bull crap. But the truth is, love is hard. Love hurts. Love out of balance leads to obsession, isolation, depression, and pain. We often mistake love as forgiveness or turning away from anger, but that's love out of balance. Love in balance is righteous anger and being held accountable. Love requires bravery and fierceness.

Don't fall into the simple thinking that love cures all and heals the world. It doesn't. If love was enough to solve all problems,

13. Crowley, *Book of Law*, 13.

Mary Magdalene would have lived a very different life. But by working with her, we can learn to live a life more love-filled. This idea shouldn't be heretical, and yet, it totally is.

OF ROSES AND JARS

One of the myths that is part of Mary Magdalene's legend is related to the death of Jesus. It is told that where her tears fell to the ground as she wept, roses grew. And as she ran from her homeland and traveled to France, anywhere her tears touched the earth, roses grew. Or so they say. Mary Magdalene has become entwined with the mythos of roses because of this part of her story.

There is also the alabaster jar, a tool of healing, wealth, and prosperity. The roses and the jar are two signs of the power and wisdom of Mary Magdalene.

Roses

Roses are known as the flower of love. The petals, the hips, the waters, and the oils made from roses are all ingredients in love spells. And yet, even the flower of love comes with a price. Have you ever been pricked by a rose thorn? If you've ever picked a rose, you likely have. Love comes with a price—and sometimes a little pain. No one knows this lesson better than Mary Magdalene.

Where Mary Magdalene's tears fell, roses grew from the ground. There are stories across the planet of entities, deities, and other ethereal beings crying or bleeding and then a sacred or special plant growing where the tears or blood fell. Each of us has a special relationship—or the potential for a special relationship—with green bloods, also known as plants.

So, considering that, I ask you, dear heretic, what plants would grow from your falling tears? What is your scent? What aromas bring you peace, joy, happiness, and inspiration?

You may already know your plant allies, or maybe this concept is a totally new one to you. Either way, let's take some time to connect to a special green blood.

⬱ Meeting Your Plant Ally ⬱

Plant allies provide us with a lot of personal information. Plant allies show up when we are ill, and they have the medicine our bodies need. They offer information on where we may need growth or healing. Plant allies guide us the same way animal allies, ancestors, and deities might. These allies can also help us connect more deeply to the natural world.

Perform the following working when you can be alone for up to thirty minutes. You will want to be undisturbed, so leave your phone in another room. Sit or lie down and let your body be as comfortable as possible.

Trance: Breathe deeply and allow yourself to relax. Focus on a deep inhale, calling in the wisdom of the world. (Pause.) Focus on a deep exhale, releasing what doesn't serve you in this moment. (Pause.) Repeat this inhale of wisdom and exhale of release. Take your time and breathe slowly, allowing each breath to bring your awareness deeper and relaxing your body. (Long pause.)

Shift your awareness by opening your witch's eye, that third eye that sits just above and between your normal seeing eyes. When this eye is fully open, you see before you a vast garden.

Every plant that has ever existed lives in this garden. You can hear the buzzing of bees and see birds flitting about. There is a heady scent of flowers, vegetables, herbs, and greens all mixing and mingling, wafting all around you.

Move through this garden. Just let your feet carry you. Look around and take in the sights and scents. Feel the energy of the plants around you. (Pause.)

As you wander, you will notice one plant on the path that calls to you. It will look a little brighter, smell a little stronger, and feel like a plant that you want to have a conversation with. It might even feel like it is calling to you. (Pause.)

When this plant makes itself known, sit down in this magickal garden and begin a conversation. Ask this plant what it is and what it wants to be called. See what wisdom it holds for you. (Long pause.)

Your time in the garden is limited for now, but you can come back to this garden at any time. Take a moment to thank your green blood ally. Ask what it needs you to do in your normal life to honor it. (Long pause.)

When you are ready, turn away from your ally and begin to wander through this lush and vibrant garden again. As you do, allow that witch's eye to close back down to its normal state.

Focus again on your breathing. Take notice of the room your body is in. Feel the clothes on your skin. Tap your body's edges and place your hands on the top of your head. Say your name out loud three times and slowly open your eyes.

Welcome back!

Now that you know one of your plant allies, you can begin to deepen this relationship. Learn about the plant. Grow the plant. If it's safe to do so, eat it, burn it, or make it into a tea. Take it in in as many forms as possible. Foster this relationship; you will be amazed by what you learn.

Jars

The other (in)famous tool of Mary Magdalene is the alabaster jar. In the stories, Jesus is anointed by a woman holding an alabaster jar filled with expensive spikenard perfume. In most translations of the Bible, the woman who performs this act is unnamed, but many believe it to be Mary Magdalene. This is an important act; it is another place in the stories that connects her to the power of priestess. She anoints a holy man with holy oils. A blessing from the goddess.

In the Bible, Mary Magdalene anoints Jesus with expensive spikenard perfume, pouring it over his head. The other followers give her a hard time, upset because the perfume was pricey and could have been sold to help the poor. Jesus responds, "Why do you trouble the woman? For she has done a beautiful thing to me. For you always have the poor with you, but you will not always have me. In pouring this ointment on my body she has done it to prepare me for burial."[14]

There is so much that we could dive into in this passage. In fact, biblical scholars have done just that ever since the Bible was written. But I am not a biblical scholar, and I am uninterested in the words of Jesus. I am much more interested in the actions of Mary Magdalene. She has much to teach us from this simple action of anointing.

First, let's look at anointing. Anointing is the process of smearing or rubbing holy (aka magickal) oil onto a person to confer religious meaning or blessing, or to give holy office. Here Mary Magdalene offers a holy blessing to the most holy of men. This suggests that she had religious power. In the writing, Jesus himself acknowledges this fact.

---

14. Matthew 26: 10–13 (Revised Standard Version).

Next, let's look at spikenard perfume. Everything in a myth is significant. All mythological stories are filled with hidden gems of information; spikenard is an interesting piece of the puzzle. At the time of this story, spikenard was an expensive perfume because the plant didn't grow in the region. It was only possible to procure through trade. Spikenard has a woody, amber-like scent, and it was a prized scent in the time of Mary Magdalene.

In magick, spikenard is a plant used to maintain health and fidelity. Interesting choice for a woman to pour spikenard oil over the head of her beloved. We don't know if Mary Magdalene made this choice as a magickal act of spellworking for fidelity or if this was just what was on hand, but the implications of this specific oil are intriguing, to say the least.

Have you ever anointed another person? It is a deeply intimate and powerful act. To take a blessed oil or perfume and put it on another human's body connects you in a deeply spiritual manner. It's like saying "This oil is holy, and by placing it on your body I acknowledge you are also holy. And in performing this holy act, I must also acknowledge that I too am holy." It's truly beautiful. This is the power Mary Magdalene shows us.

As heretics, we have the ability and responsibility to show others their holiness. Overculture has us all believing that holiness is out there somewhere, up in the sky or something. But holiness is right here! Touch your heart. Seriously, put your hand on your chest right now and feel your heart beating—that's holy.

The thought of you reading these words and experiencing your holiness right this moment brings me to tears. Heretics need more of this. There needs to be more recognition of holiness in the world around us all the time.

Do you realize how many people don't know they are holy or take it for granted? Most of them. Heretics must show people their holiness, wake them up, shake them up, and help reconnect them to the power of themselves. This is no small task.

Okay. What the heck does any of this have to do with jars?

ᏏᎥ Making Your Own Alabaster Jar ᏏᎥ

So, now what? Haven't you seen any of the jokes about witches and jars? Here's the joke: Jars hold spells, herbs, potions, magickal waters, and so much more. Witches do love us some jars. And really, any heretic worth their salt needs to have healing unguents and holy oils, which means now is the perfect time to make your own alabaster jar.

For this working, use any jar with a sturdy lid. You might want to use a smaller bottle rather than a jar. When you find the right bottle, decorate the outside of it. Allow yourself to be creative. You might want to use paints or pens for writing on glass. You could also decoupage images on the outside of the glass. Make it beautiful.

This container will hold a blessing oil that you can use to anoint yourself, your friends, your ritual tools, or anything really. As a heretic, as a witch, it is important you have your own holy blessing oil. I'm including some holy oil recipes here, but consider this a jumping-off point to creating holy oils that connect to your special plant allies and favorite scents.

As with anything in this book, do not use any ingredients you are allergic to. If you are uncertain about your reaction to any of the ingredients listed, please skip them. Herbology is something that needs to be studied. Herbs are medicine, and it is dangerous to attempt to dabble in medicine when you don't know the science of it. Herbs and essential oils can harm you if you don't know what you are doing. Always dilute essential oils, and never take them internally.

For any sacred oil creation, you need to start with a base oil.

✦ ✦ ✦ Base Oils ✦ ✦ ✦

All essential oil blends and perfume oils use a base or carrier oil. Using essential oils directly on your skin is dangerous and can harm you. Essential oils are harsh and need to be diluted or mellowed out with a base oil.

A base oil should be one with very little flavor and scent so it doesn't overpower your essential oils. And there are lots to choose from.

Almond Oil: This is a very popular base oil because it is so lightweight. However, it does have a stronger nutty scent, which may alter the scent of the essential oils you use.

Apricot Kernel Oil: This oil comes from apricot seeds and can be beneficial for folks with sensitive skin. It has a very soft, sweet aroma.

Argan Oil: This oil comes from argan trees. It is traditionally used on the skin and in food. It has a very light nutty scent and is hydrating for the skin.

Grapeseed Oil: This oil is a byproduct of wine making. It is very lightweight and absorbs into the skin easily. It has very little scent.

Jojoba Oil: This is made from the seeds of the jojoba plant. It is light and absorbs easily into the skin because it is very similar to the skin's natural oils. It has a light nutty scent.

Olive Oil: This oil is very moisturizing on the skin. It does have a strong fruity scent, which can interfere with the scent of essential oils.

The following recipes are intended to be made using two ounces of base oil. Increase drop amounts based on the amount of oil you want to make. First put the essential oils in the jar, then fill the jar or bottle with your chosen carrier oil.

Keep in mind that oils do go bad. A little bit of an essential oil goes a long way. It is better to make a small amount and need to make more than have it go rancid because you weren't able to use it all.

HOLY OIL #1
6 drops frankincense essential oil
6 drops myrrh essential oil
2 drops sandalwood essential oil

HOLY OIL #2
4 drops sweet orange essential oil
2 drops ginger essential oil
2 drops cedar essential oil

HOLY OIL #3
4 drops rosemary essential oil
4 drops rose perfume essential oil
2 drops jasmine essential oil

Pour your oil into your decorated jar. Use this oil to anoint yourself. You can do this by putting a small amount of oil on your fingertips and intentionally touching your body. One traditional place to anoint is at your third eye—the location of your witch's eye. But you could also anoint your pulse points (wrists and behind the ears), you heart, your solar plexus, the palms of your hands, the soles of your feet, or anywhere else you may feel called.

Anoint yourself every morning. Anoint your friends when you hang out. Anoint ritual participants. But always anoint with consent!

Walking while Lost

Mary Magdalene didn't always know the way. Often, she had only her wits and intuition to guide her. Here's something a bit controversial: Your relationship with your own intuition is a relationship of trust and love. Perhaps this is the most important lesson from Mary Magdalene. How do you love and trust yourself?

Learning to love yourself has been an important part of the self-help movement. The idea that you need to be able to love yourself before you can truly love others is a big one. But this concept has taken some fire and received pushback. There are many who call this concept "toxic positivity." Folks counter this statement with the idea that sometimes all you can do is love someone else, especially when you can't love yourself.

What if—take a breath with me here—what if allowing yourself to love someone else *is* loving yourself?

Let me expand on this. I have generalized anxiety. There are times I really dislike myself. When I'm struggling to stay calm—for no apparent reason or because I'm triggered—it is very frustrating. In these moments, attempting to love myself, calm myself, or do anything reasonably helpful rarely works.

Sometimes though, I can go hang out with my daughter, play with the cat, have a conversation with my husband, or pet the dog. Sometimes I listen to an audiobook, paint, or dance. I shift my focus to things I love. These are ways I love myself, even if I might not like myself very much. Self-care is loving yourself. And truly knowing yourself.

Loving yourself is listening to your intuition. What is it that you need? What does your gut tell you? And how do you respond to serve that need?

Traveling to the Realm of Mary Magdalene

So many times in my life I've wondered what it would have been like to live during specific historical moments. The life and times of Mary Magdalene is one of them. Priestess of an ancient goddess, lover, wife, heretic, and force of love. What an interesting woman she would have been.

A visit with Mary Magdalene can help you find answers to love, mystery, connection, and so much more. The following ritual will help you connect to her power directly.

Supplies: A vase of roses, a strong incense like myrrh or frankincense, and a small bowl of salt water.

Set Up: Create a simple altar with the roses in the center. Keep the incense and bowl of water close by.

Before you begin, sprinkle yourself with the salted water. Use this as a cleansing. Visualize the salt water clearing any negative energy or distraction. Anoint your third eye with this water. Anoint your heart and the back of your neck.

Say, "Mary of Magdalene, I call to you. Open the way to your rose-covered temple. Show me the way to your heart."

When you feel ready, light the incense and get comfortable, either sitting or lying down.

Trance: Breathe in slowly, counting to four. Then hold for a count of two. Exhale for a count of eight and hold for a count of two. Repeat this process—inhale for four, hold for two, exhale for eight, and hold for two—over and over again. (Pause.)

Take notice of your heart. Feel the beating force of life that sits in the middle of your chest. This place is the center of your emotional energy. As your heart beats, take notice of the energy here. Does your heart center feel open and clear? Can you breathe into this space? (Pause.)

Shift your focus to the edges of your body and allow them to gradually and slowly expand. With each breath you take, the edges of you become wider and wider. From this place of expanded awareness, open your witch's eye.

With your witch's eye open, you see before you a path leading to a hillside temple, built into the walls of the mountain. The twisting path is surrounded by huge rose bushes. These roses are in all colors, with buds, full blossoms, and hips all available at once. There are bees happily buzzing past the thorny bushes and small birds flitting all about you. Take a step, one foot in front of the other, and begin to follow this rose-filled path up the mountainside. (Pause.)

Its gradual upward climb is easy, and you follow the sandy path up, up, up. (Pause.) As you move along the path, take note of your surroundings. Pay attention to anything odd or interesting that makes itself known to you. Continue to walk along, one foot in front of the other toward the temple.

You reach the large and majestic doorway of the temple, carved right into the mountain, big and impressive. The doors are open wide. You can feel a coolness coming from deep within, coating your warm skin. You can smell the roses, but now, with the temple doors open, you can also smell the heady scent of incense.

Out of the open doorway steps Mary Magdalene. She is beautiful and strong. She walks down the steps of the temple, coming closer to you and extending her hand in greeting.

What is in your heart right now? This is what you should speak to her about. Take some time to speak with Mary Magdalene. Ask her the secret questions you hold in your heart and see what wisdom she holds for you. (Long pause.)

Before your time in this realm comes to an end, Mary Magdalene reaches out her hand and places it over your heart. A rosy glow engulfs you. It is warm and comforting. This rosy glow melts something you didn't even know was frozen. There is a shift and a release. Take a breath. (Pause.)

Offer your gratitude to Mary Magdalene and say goodbye to her for now, knowing that you can return here at any time. (Pause.)

Mary Magdalene walks back into the temple as you turn around and follow the desert path away from this sacred site. Step by step, you move back through the sandy path in the rose bushes. As you walk your witch's eye begins to close, returning to its normal state.

Take three deep breaths and feel the warm glow from your heart center. Feel the edges of your body and place your hands on the top of your head. Say your name out loud three times and slowly open your eyes.

Welcome back!

Pick up one of the roses and smell the blossom. Speak your thanks to Mary Magdalene out loud and write down anything important or interesting from your visit.

BEING A HERETIC WITH MARY MAGDALENE

It's time to be a heretic. It's time. In *her* time, Mary Magdalene understood this. It was time then, too. There have been pivotal moments throughout history where a heretic had to step up, and if they hadn't, who the heck knows where we would be right now. Goddess bless the heretics.

Mary Magdalene shows us the path to heretical teachings from a place of love. This is not a message to love your enemy. Nope, I'm not on board with that. However, I am a fan of loving yourself, taking care of yourself, and loving your friends, family, pets, children, lovers, communities, and the spirits of the land. Love the things that deserve your love. Forget all the rest.

You may not imagine Mary Magdalene saying "Forget all the rest," but think about that for a moment. She followed her beloved through the desert, throwing away everything she "should" have been doing as a woman of the time. She shared the teachings of love and change. She spoke truth to power just like Jesus, speaking of feeding the poor, taking care of the sick, driving out the bill collectors, and keeping safe space for the most vulnerable populations.

Many modern people look down their noses at the past and think that all those ancient folks just had old-fashioned values; old-fashioned ways of thinking. We modern people think we know better than that. But do we really? Take a good look at the world right now.

Love, change, truth, taking care of others; these should not be heretical values. These should be human values. And yet, there are plenty of places where these are not common values.

Are you on board, heretic? Or are you happy with the status quo? Mary Magdalene shows us the way to have a strong, brave, rebellious heart while still having deep love, compassion, and care as our driving force.

> ✦ ✦ ✦ **Heretic Contemplation** ✦ ✦ ✦
>
> Where in your life can you see yourself connecting with divine love like Mary Magdalene? What comes up for you when you ponder the concept of love? Take out your journal and write the word LOVE across the top. Let yourself free write on this word. Write at least one full page.
>
> Set down this writing and go do something else. Don't return to your writing for at least one hour. Then read over what you wrote and reflect.
>
> How can you share your love with the world? Write down one step you can take right now.

CHAPTER 10

JEANNE D'ARC

Now we come to the story of a young woman who was labeled a heretic and died as a heretic. You might be wondering, *Who the heck is Jeanne D'Arc? I've never heard of this person.* You likely know her by her anglicized name, Joan of Arc. However, to honor her native language, I will be only referring to her as Jeanne D'Arc (pronounced zhahn dark).

One of my all-time favorite quotes is a misquote that comes from Jeanne D'Arc: "I am not afraid ... I was born to do this." What she actually said was, "I do not fear ... It was for this I was born."[15] However, her misquote has taken on a life of its own. I've used this quote many times myself when I needed to remember my own badassery. And that's just one of the things that Jeanne helps us with.

Born around 1412, Jeanne D'Arc was a remarkable girl from a rather basic background. She could not read or write and was raised as a devout Catholic in northeastern France. During her entire life there was a long and terrible war going on between

---

15. Kennedy, "Joan of Arc Quote."

France and England. The region of France Jeanne lived in was occupied by England and many of her neighbors were forced to leave their homes due to raids because of it.

At the age of thirteen, Jeanne started to hear voices. She believed the voices came from God and the three saints that were part of her local church. At first these voices (and visions) told her how to live a chaste and good life. As time went on, though, she started receiving much bigger messages—like how to save France from the English. The voices of her saints gave specific instructions on what she needed to do, including learning how to ride a horse and basic fighting skills. The most important step she had to take, according to her visions, was to get Charles, the Prince of France, in place as France's rightful king.

When she was sixteen years old, Jeanne's father attempted to arrange a wedding for her, convinced that marriage might calm her down and bring stability into her life. Jeanne wanted nothing to do with that plan. Instead, she went to the local courts and convinced them she should not be forced into a marriage. Can you imagine the cheek?!

Later that same year, Jeanne convinced her uncle to take her to the nearby stronghold of those loyal to Prince Charles. At the stronghold, she requested a retinue that could get her an audience with Charles. She was initially thrown out. So she took to the streets, speaking so passionately about Charles and how he would liberate the people of France that she gathered up quite the band of followers for herself. Eventually, the folks she gathered were able to convince the leadership to help her.

Of course, it helped that there was a popular local prophecy that said a virgin girl would save France from the war. Many believed Jeanne was that person. I mean, religious prophecy helps, right?

She chopped off her hair and dressed as a boy in order to make the two-week long, perilous journey through enemy lines to get to Charles. Once she arrived, she was able to gain a private audience with Charles. Charles knew why Jeanne was coming to speak with him, so he disguised himself as one of his courtiers to test her discernment. She immediately called him out as Prince Charles, and he then honored her request for a private conversation.

Obviously, no one knows for sure what was said between Jeanne and Charles during their private chat. She was asked over and over again during her trials what she said. All she would reveal was that she had personal information about him that was given to her by God and encouraged Charles to honor her wishes.[16]

Charles was convinced of her power. So much so that when Jeanne left, she took with her an army to fend off the Siege of Orleans. She wore white armor atop a white horse with the soldiers behind her, never having fought in a battle before. And although she was wounded in the battle, they won!

Now the rumors and talk started to spread about this girl. After Orleans, the French soldiers pushed forward and took back another city from the English. Jeanne encouraged Charles to continue moving forward and take back Paris. But after his official coronation that took place after the battle of Orleans, Charles VII started to waver in his support of the girl. There was talk amongst his counselors that she was getting too powerful and had too much support from the people, perhaps even more than he did. A big problem for a newly crowned king in the middle of a war.

Jeanne pushed on to Paris without Charles by her side. She was convinced the people of the city would join her in the fight against the English, but they didn't. It was her first major failure

---

16. Maid of Heaven Foundation, "Joan of Arc & Charles VII."

and a big blow to her mystique. But Jeanne continued to fight for a year, helping plan sieges and attacks and being a shining beacon of hope for the people of France.

Finally, during another siege, Jeanne was wounded and thrown from her horse. It was at this point she was captured by English soldiers. She was accused of over seventy crimes, including witchcraft, dressing like a man, and heresy. Charles, worried about making a political mistake, distanced himself from Jeanne, and the French did nothing to help get her released.

After a year of captivity, Jeanne finally signed a confession. Funnily enough, they didn't care about her admitting to any of the charges except for one. They wanted her to admit that she had received no divine guidance. There is some debate as to why she finally signed the confession—many believe it was fear of being burned—but sign the confession she did. Signing the confession meant she would spend life in prison, but she would not be burned at the stake.

However, the very next day, she defied her captors, wore men's clothing again, and said she did hear the voice of God: "Everything I have done I have done at the instruction of my voices."[17] It was this final heretical act that brought the death sentence against her. In May of 1431, Jeanne was burned at the stake.

Her popularity only increased after her death. Twenty years later, Charles VII cleared her posthumously of any charges. It wasn't until the early 1900s that Jeanne D'Arc was officially canonized by the Catholic church and became the patron saint of France.

When I think of Jeanne D'Arc, I think about this young girl with fire in her blood. What kind of magick so possessed this

---

17. North, *Joan of Arc*, 64.

young girl that she was able to lead an entire army during a time when women did no such thing? She was fueled by the power of her relationship to God, and that relationship gave her more power than any other woman of the time.

Jeanne was well known for having a temper and dressing down knights of a higher social class than she was. She held so strongly to her convictions that nothing and no one stood in her way. She was never afraid, and even if she was, she did the thing anyway.

This is a woman who didn't know how to read or write. She was born to poor farming parents. But she took the world by storm. She convinced hundreds of powerful people to believe in her, take her advice on war strategy, and follow her into battle. She must have had the gift of the gab. I wish we knew her astrological chart!

Jeanne never wavered on her principles. Even after being imprisoned for a year, she pushed back against her oppressors. She is an honorable heretic.

OF BRAVERY AND SWORDS

Jeanne was unbelievably brave. She was a peasant raised on a simple farm and, somehow, she managed to rally armies. Personally, I cannot imagine witnessing the terrors of battle, let alone standing at the front of them and helping organize them. She heard her true calling and never let her faith waiver.

One thing said about bravery is that it's not the absence of fear, but experiencing fear and doing the thing anyway. No doubt Jeanne had moments of fear, but she never let that stop her, and her bravery became a force that inspired others.

The question I've always had about Jeanne D'Arc is how did she learn to fight? She was raised on a farm by a devoutly Catholic mother. I can't image there was much time for sparring and training with a sword. And this is true, she didn't know how to fight. But she wasn't totally removed from dangers of battle. With her, we have another example of the myth becoming bigger than the reality.

Jeanne wasn't on the front lines and didn't fight herself. Really, how could she? She was never trained. Written history tells us she was a standard bearer, carrying a flag of religious symbols that she had created. She was there to give strength to the knights and to be a beacon of hope. But even standing on a distant hill, she would have seen the harshness of fighting, she would have smelled the blood of the dying, and she would have witnessed the death of the men she had called to the fight. War is ugly and harsh. These are the kinds of experiences that change a person. Even though she was wounded in her very first battle, it didn't stop her from going to the next one and the next one after that.

It is recorded in court documents that Jeanne received battle visions and details ahead of time from her saints and God. She is said to have known ahead of time she was going to be wounded in battle and that she would be captured, but this didn't stop her from putting herself on the line.[18] She went into battle anyway.

Jeanne D'Arc can show us how to be brave. She can show us how to keep going, even if we don't think we can. And even though she didn't use the sword in battle, she can help us pick up a sword as a tool of clarity and change.

---

18. North, *Joan of Arc*, 60.

Bravery

Heretics must be brave. So much of living a heretical life is standing up for what you believe in, standing up against oppression, and pushing back against cultural lies. This means you will often have to say the scary thing, do the scary thing, and make yourself uncomfortable.

Comfort is not a bad thing, but it can lead to complacency. Complacency can lead to apathy, and before you know it, we have fascists running the country. You could argue that all the women in this book are shining examples of bravery and you would not be wrong, but there is something about the story of Jeanne that makes *me* feel brave.

She wasn't only known for leading an army and convincing a should-be king to be her backer. She was also known to be a bit of a hothead. She would verbally dress down decorated knights who swore too much. She would chastise soldiers for skipping mass on Sundays. And she was known to chase off prostitutes from the surrounding encampments.[19] This was fueled by her unwavering Catholic faith and belief in God.

What in your life has your unwavering faith?

Don't get me wrong, this is a really hard question to answer. Honestly, I'm not sure there is anything in this world that has my unwavering faith, except for maybe the only constant is change. And I'll tell you what, that's okay.

You don't need unwavering faith to be brave. Bravery comes from somewhere else and connects us to something else.

Remember that misquote? "I am not afraid; I was born to do this."

---

19. North, *Joan of Arc*, 38–39.

What were you born to do, heretic? What makes you the rebel that you are? Why are you here?

> ✦ ✦ ✦ **What Were You Born to Do?** ✦ ✦ ✦
> • Live.
> • Be you.
>
> That's it.

You don't have to lead the armies, you don't have to start a revolution, you don't have to liberate cities and fight to the death. All you have to do is live and be you.

This is a heretical act.

Seriously, look at our current world. We are encouraged to turn our passions into side hustles. We always must be producing, creating, being a part of gig economy, and contributing. Work, work, work—even going so far as to make your play into your work. Our culture makes no time for rest, peace, tranquility, and love. It's all go, do, be, make ...

This might sound like I'm trying to say two different things here. Be heretical, be brave, be bold. And then on the other hand, be you, live, that's all. But those two things can be the *same*. If you are being you, if you are living your truth, that is an act of bravery. This is what Jeanne shows us.

Was she hearing the voice of God? Who the hell am I to say? She followed that voice's guidance and accomplished amazing things. She lived her truth; she was simply herself.

What might your life look like if you lived your truth?

BORN TO DO

What would you do if there was no way you could fail? What risk would you take, what phone call would you make, what job would you apply for, what thing would you do?

Bravery doesn't mean that you always succeed; bravery means that you try.

Six years before writing this book, a huge opportunity fell into my lap. A local esoteric shop was up for sale. Mind you, I had no experiencing running a retail business, I had not-so-great credit, and I had literally no savings, but I felt called to buy this business.

I reached out to my friends and community members. I made calls to folks I knew who owned similar businesses and asked for advice. I talked to an accountant about what I needed to know and asked them to look over the books. I didn't really know what the heck I was doing. And in all respects, it never should have worked out.

But I had also petitioned one of my deities. Synchronicity brought me a blessed and magickal piece of jewelry, and an amazing angel investor stepped out from the shadows. It all literally fell into place as if it was meant to be.

There were moments throughout the whole process when I was frozen with fear. It was a *huge* amount of money I was being loaned. There were several employees who would be depending on me for their livelihood. And did I mention that I had no idea what I was doing?

I knew in my heart, in my gut, in my soul, that I was born to do this. Instead of letting the fear and the doubt stop my actions, I just kept going.

There have been several moments in my life where I knew I was born to do the thing. And I went for it. I put myself out there. I pushed myself out of my comfort zone. No doubt you have these moments in your life too. Moments where you pushed yourself past the fear and into the bravery zone. My challenging moments did not always turn out as I would have wanted, but they always turned out okay.

So, I ask you again, what were you born to do? What would you do if you knew you could not fail?

Swords

We know now that it was unlikely Jeanne D'Arc knew how to wield a sword. However, the persistent imagery of her fighting cannot be turned away from. And in that spirit, we will work with the sword as a magickal and heretical tool gifted to us from her.

The sword is an interesting tool. I use the word *tool* very specifically. Yes, the sword is a weapon, but what is a weapon if not a tool?

Many modern esoteric practices incorporate the use of the sword in their rituals. The sword shows up as one of the suits in tarot. It is a symbol of clarity, discernment, and communication.

When I'm doing a tarot reading for a client and a Swords card shows up, I always take it as a reminder that something needs to be cut away or cleared up. The power of the sword is more than something that inflicts wounds or kills. It can cut away what no longer serves, cut lines in the sand, create boundaries, and remove what is dying.

Knowing how to best use a sword in your own circumstances can only be done by using discernment. Discernment is the most powerful tool of any witch or heretic. Discernment is the ability to judge well. To make a clear and smart decision. When you can wield the tool of discernment, it helps you use the tool of the sword.

⚜ Making Decisions with Swords ⚜

There are plenty of moments when we find ourselves at a crossroads, when we have more than one choice to make and we are uncertain how to proceed. Use this ritual to help you pick the right path.

Supplies: An Ace of Swords tarot card (or the image of an Ace of Swords tarot card), strips of paper with a pen, a large bowl, lemongrass incense, a glass-encased white candle, a cauldron or other firesafe container, and a lighter.

Set Up: Place the candle in the center of your space and light it. Lean the tarot card against it. Light the incense and have the papers, bowl, and firesafe container nearby.

When you are ready, light the incense and keep it burning. Take a moment to study the tarot card. Feel your energy connect with the card. The Ace of Swords is connected to clarity and focus, clear communication, and fresh starts. Breathe deeply and imagine clear winds of clarity whipping around you. Imagine the air as a sword that can slice right through any mental confusion and bring you the answer you seek.

Think about a situation that makes you feel uncertain about how to proceed. Write down all of your options for next steps on the strips of paper. For this ritual, the more options, the better. Write down everything—the good, the bad, the totally impossible, the plausible, and the easy. A slip of paper for each one. Then put the slips of paper into the bowl.

Swirl all the strips around and say, "I seek clarity, I seek truth, I seek wisdom. I use the tool of discernment and the power of the sword to clear the way and easily show me the best choice."

Without looking, select two of the strips of paper from the bowl. Read both of your options. Then pick one. Yep, you only get to pick one. The one that you don't select gets immediately burned. Light it and place it in your firesafe container. Release that option from your heart as you watch the paper burn to ashes.

Set the strip you've picked aside and pick out two more. Repeat the process until you have a small pile of the strips that you've selected.

Place the selected strips all back in the bowl, swirl the bowl around, and say, "I seek clarity, I seek truth, I seek wisdom. I use the tool of discernment and the power of the sword to clear the way and easily show me the best choice."

Pick up two of the strips of paper. Read both of your options. Then pick one. The one that you don't select gets burned.

Repeat the entire process until you end up with just one strip of paper and you have your answer!

Walking while Leading

Not all of us are cut out for the leadership role. Not all of us want leadership. Jeanne D'Arc was born to be a leader, but there are lots of other leaders in her story. There is Charles, who took a chance on a strange young farm girl. There is her uncle, who believed in her so much that he risked taking her to the local leaders and putting their family's lives at risk. There is the English leadership that decided to pursue accusing Jeanne of wearing men's clothing in court, which had never been done before.

Heretics become leaders. Sometimes we are ready and happy to take that on. Sometimes we resist all the way through it. But remember our discussion about power? Healthy leadership isn't about power-over. Healthy leadership is about finding the best way through.

Jeanne wasn't trained in leadership skills. There was no HR department to check in with or weekend workshops to teach her how to deal with difficult people. She didn't always know the right thing to do, but again, she always kept moving forward. She always took the risk.

Whether you decide you want to step into a leadership role or whether you want to avoid leadership at all costs, it doesn't really matter. We all need to learn how to support healthy leadership.

❧ Traveling to the Realm of Jeanne D'Arc ☙

Jeanne D'Arc helps us to connect to our bravery and also our destiny. Jeanne knew what she was born to do. Her calling was clear, and her bravery stemmed from that understanding. In connecting with her, we can find answers to our own direction and learn how to stay brave in the face of adversity.

Supplies: A sword (if you don't have one, use the largest knife you've got), a glass of wine or grape juice, and a glass-encased candle of any color.

Set Up: Lay your swords down in front of where you will perform this ritual. Place the glass of wine nearby and light the candle. Sit in front of the space you have created.

Before setting out on the trance, take some time in quiet meditative reflection. Where do you need a boost in bravery? Where are you feeling disconnected from your destiny? Find clarity on what you might want to talk to Jeanne D'Arc about.

Say: "I call to you, Jeanne D'Arc, the patron saint of France. I call to you, Jeanne D'Arc, visionary and brave soul. Help me to find my own bravery, help me to see the best way forward. I call to you, Jeanne D'Arc."

Lie or sit with your spine straight in as comfortable a position as possible.

Trance: Allow yourself to breathe slowly, in and out, aware of your body. Feel the air as it comes into your lungs and pause for a moment before letting the air leave your body. Focus for a moment on the in and out of air flow. (Long pause.)

As you relax and sink into your breathing, notice yourself being surrounded by a cloud. A soft, warm cloud begins to form around your body. This cloud begins to lift you up off the ground, and you feel yourself held in the warm embrace of this magickal cloud. (Pause.)

The cloud continues to move up, up, up, rising up above your space. The cloud slowly lifts you further into the sky. It carries you up above the clouds, keeping you warm and safe as it starts to move forward. (Pause.)

The cloud gently carries you forward, moving and moving, when the direction gently changes. That magickal cloud begins to lower. Coming down, down, down, back down through the cloud cover. You are held, safe and warm, by the cloud.

Gently, you feel your feet touch the ground and the cloud begins to dissipate. You see before you a simple church in the French countryside. The rolling hills around you are lush with green, and the church stands as if glowing in the sunlight.

The doors of the church open and Jeanne D'Arc emerges. She is dressed in her perfect white knight garb with her hair cut short. She proudly carries her banner, placing it into the earth right outside the church doors. You can hear the fabric rippling in the wind. She walks toward you and gestures for you to come and speak with her.

Move forward and take this time to speak with Jeanne. Ask for her advice regarding your own bravery and see what wisdom this heretic has for you. (Long pause.)

Your time in this place is limited. Take a few more moments to say anything else in your heart or to ask this warrior anything else you need to know. (Long pause.)

Remember that you can return here to see Jeanne D'Arc at any time, but for now you must take your leave. If you haven't already, offer your gratitude to Jeanne, say your goodbyes, and watch as she turns and steps back into her beloved church.

As she walks away, the cloud returns to you, forming around you sturdy, strong, and firm. This warm cloud begins to lift you off the ground, rising up from the French countryside and returning you to your place in the world.

The cloud rises up, up, up, carrying you safely. The cloud rises above the cloud line in the sky and begins to move forward. The journey is shorter this time, as it knows exactly where it is headed. You feel the cloud shift, bringing you back down, down, down. This warm cloud lowers you right back to your body.

Take a deep breath and feel this cloud dissipate. Take another deep breath and feel the edges of your body become firm and solid. Use your hands to tap the edges of your body. Place your hands on the top of your head and speak your name out loud three times. Slowly open your eyes and take in your surroundings.

Welcome back!

Pick up the glass of wine and raise it. Say, "For you, Jeanne. Thank you. Hail and farewell." Set the glass down.

Write down anything that feels important to track from your journey. Then blow out the candle and say, "Thank you, Jeanne D'Arc. I am not afraid."

When you feel ready, take the glass of wine outside and pour it in a wild place.

Being a Heretic with Jeanne D'Arc

For me, the message of Jeanne D'Arc is clear: Let no one stand in your way. Jeanne didn't care if the person she spoke with was a religious leader, a decorated knight, or the freakin' king of France. It didn't matter who they were supposed to be, she knew her message. She knew what was right and she stuck by her beliefs.

Jeanne helps us when we are afraid, yes, but she can also show us what is worth being afraid of. I'll tell you, it's not very many things. Don't be afraid of titles, of supposed "power," like being a king. She shows us none of that matters when your message is pure.

When it comes time to fight and fully open your heretical heart, Jeanne leads the way and screams at the top of her lungs for the charge to move forward.

✦ ✦ ✦ Heretic Contemplation ✦ ✦ ✦

How are you like Jeanne D'Arc? How are you nothing like Jeanne D'Arc? Where in your life do you need to step up your bravery?

What are your big goals and dreams? How do you imagine yourself being a heretic? What in life would make your heart full of pride and joy? Heretics take bold action. Now is the time for you to take bold action.

Pick one thing that you want to do. Maybe it's an item from your bucket list. Maybe it's a crazy dream that you never really expected to achieve. Maybe it is something that would make your life a little bit easier. Perhaps you want to go back to school, or visit Hawaii, or become a race car driver. Maybe you want to audition for a play, or schedule a massage, or get a pet. It doesn't matter what your goal is; just pick one.

Set this book down right now and take one step toward making that happen.

Do it right now. Go.

CHAPTER 11

SALOME

Salome (pronounced sal-oh-may) is a woman in the New Testament of the Bible, but she has become bigger than the short excerpt of her from that book. She has grown in popularity through art and writing in the many years since she may have lived—even up to the early 1900s, when a one-act play (and then opera) was written about her.[20] Due to these modern writings, Salome has become synonymous with the femme fatal, or as a symbol of the power of a woman's desirability.

What we know from brief mention of her in the New Testament is that she was the stepdaughter of Herod Antipas. Antipas was a tetrarch, a Roman-appointed ruler of Galilee, in an area of current-day Palestine. In the Gospels of Mark and Matthew, Salome shows up in the story told about Herod Antipas and his imprisonment of John the Baptist, who was quite the heretical character himself.[21]

---

20. *Encyclopaedia Britannica Online*, s.v. "Salome," accessed May 7, 2021, https://www.britannica.com/biography/Salome-stepdaughter-of -Herod-Antipas.

21. Mark 6:14–29 and Matthew 14: 1–12 (RSV).

John the Baptist was a religious heretic and leader, baptizing people in the name of God and telling people they too could have a personal relationship with God, no intermediary necessary. He was a cousin of Jesus and had many enemies of his own. John the Baptist had also publicly spoken out against the marriage between Herod Antipas and his second wife, Salome's mother, Herodias. He proclaimed their marriage was invalid and went against Mosaic law. These declarations against the ruler led to John's arrest. You don't talk shit about the tetrarch and his new wife and get away with it, apparently.

Because John the Baptist had a large following and was believed by many to be a prophet, Herod was afraid to kill him. Scholars debate if he was afraid for superstitious or political reasons, but I would wager it was a bit of both. However, Herodias was not okay with keeping John alive. She felt slighted by this man in a very public way and wanted him dead. It also didn't hurt that John was out in the world, performing heretical acts, and Herod needed some excuse to get him off the streets.

In one of the modern versions of the tale, Salome was in love with John the Baptist, but he had spurned her advances. (Based on the historical information, there is no way to know if this version speaks to any truth or not. It's pretty unlikely that the two would have known each other, but it does make for a dramatic tale.) The story goes on to describe Herod's birthday celebration, where Salome was asked to dance for the gathered guests. There is no description of this dance, but biblical stories tell us Herod requested it. He cajoled her into doing a dance and said that in return for this birthday gift, he would give her anything she wished.

In the one-act opera called *Salome*, created by Richard Strauss, the story is a little sultrier. Salome dances for the party, and as she does so, she inflames her stepfather's passions. In response to his desire, he offers her anything she wishes if she will dance more, just for him. She accepts this offer, and once the dance is complete, she calls for the head of John the Baptist on a platter, which is the same ending as the original biblical story. Adaptations added drama and sensuality to the tale, but the outcome was always the same: the death of John the Baptist.

Richard Strauss adapted his opera from Oscar Wilde's one-act play called *Salome*. These two adaptations of the Salome story have fictionally expanded on this alluring death payment dance. You may have heard of the Dance of the Seven Veils, which is what Salome's dance was called. This comes directly from the Wilde and Strauss version of a much older, much blander Bible story.

The drama, the intrigue, and the sensuality of the Dance of the Seven Veils is a part of the tale that seems so much more interesting than anything from the original biblical version. In modern imagination, the Dance of the Seven Veils has become a burlesque striptease performance, where the seven veils are the removal of seven layers of clothing. Little is left to the imagination by the end of the dancing, but the sensual reveal has become the stuff of legends.

Salome and the Dance of the Seven Veils has taken on the symbology of sexuality, desire, and the power of seduction. Whether it is because of her unrequited love, to defend her mother's honor, or—as described in some versions of the story—as prompted *by* her mother, Salome has become the sexy dancing powerhouse that many aspire to be. Imagine the powerful, saucy hip shakes that would lead a powerful ruler to take the head of a prisoner!

In reality, the story of Salome is more than a sexy dance, although there's nothing wrong with that. Her story is also one of female scapegoats and intrigue.

Politically, Herod needed John the Baptist out of the way. He was a dangerous man changing the landscape of the culture at the time. Herod had to look out for his people, and he had to keep Rome happy. That was a difficult challenge. But again, politically—and perhaps a little superstitiously—he wasn't ready or willing to put the man to death. What is a tetrarch to do?

Conversely, stories paint Herod's wife, Herodias, as a plotting and conniving woman who would even use her daughter to manipulate her husband. She becomes a gross Lady McBeth–type character, throwing her daughter into the arms of her husband to get what she wants and to make sure her standing in society isn't damaged.

Which brings us to Salome herself. Was she an unsuspecting innocent who just wanted to provide a dance of celebration for her stepfather? Was she a manipulated daughter whose sexuality was being used by her own plotting mother? Was she a wounded girl in love who wanted revenge for rejection? Was she a devious sexpot who manipulated her stepfather?

Who knows?

The "truth" of Salome's life and motivations will never be known. But the energy of who she has become in popular culture tells us much, and it points to power we can learn from.

Of Dances and Veils

Let's go with the more modern interpretation of Salome for a moment. We can take some liberties on her story. Why not? She had a goal; she needed to achieve something outside the realm of her power—at least it seemed that way. She used what she had.

One of the things I say about witchcraft all the time is that it is a practice of using what you've got.

No one knew this better than Salome. In a time where a young woman was nothing more than a bargaining chip for those with power, Salome's options for control were very limited. But there was one thing that she had perfect control over, at least for the moment—her body.

Salome can help us connect or reconnect with our bodies. It might not be an easy relationship, but it is an important one. We only get this one body, no matter its color, size, shape, athletic level, wellness, or ability. One of the best things we can do is learn to appreciate our body.

The overculture does a really good job convincing us that we shouldn't like the skin we are in. We are bombarded with messages about how we should look. A lot of this is connected to capitalism and the patriarchy. If you are constantly striving to fulfill an impossible aesthetic, you will keep spending money on things that "they" say will help you meet the impossible goal of fitting into society's standards. The only problem is, you can never reach that goal. This has led to several generations of people who hate their bodies, have eating disorders, experience body dysmorphia, or feel disembodied. All of these things are serious issues.

Dances

Movement is important to a heretical life. We humans need to have a relationship with our bodies. After all, we only get this one.

A physical relationship with your own body may not sound like a big deal, but it really is. Many people struggle with expectations of beauty, battles with weight, and dysmorphia of all different varieties. Sometimes your body can feel like a stranger, or even the enemy, rather than your home base.

How do we move forward with a healthy body relationship when our bodies feel wrong, broken, uncomfortable, or unfamiliar? We must move it.

MOVE YOUR BODY

Move. Yep, it's as simple as that.

You don't have to know any dance steps. You don't have to follow any protocols or wear the right kind of outfits. You don't need to have an athletic build or be able to wear ballet shoes. It doesn't matter what your physical abilities are. This exercise is only about moving.

Create a playlist of songs that make you want to move your body. This list should be at least twenty minutes long, but an hour is better.

When you are ready, put on the playlist and just move. If that means you sit in a chair and move your arms, that's perfect. If you shake your hips and then sit and listen for a few minutes and then get up and shake your hips again, that's perfect. The specifics of the movement don't matter. Just move.

Let go of your thinking self. Don't worry about how you look or how you wish you could do a fancy dance. Just move. Be silly and wild. Shake it.

If you struggle with this, if you have a hard time connecting in with your body and just moving, that's okay too. Please try. And then try again in a few days. The more you can express in and with your body, the deeper your witchcraft can go.

Veils

What is a veil? On one level, a veil is a piece of clothing used to conceal or protect the face. The dictionary definition of veil specifically says this is a garment for women. A veil also disguises or conceals.

Salome used her veil, which would have likely been a regular part of her everyday clothing, to veil her intentions. She worked with what she had to shift the circumstances of her life to get what she wanted. Seems like a pretty simple definition of witchcraft to me.

We can veil things to hide our intentions and keep the truth private. We can also unveil secrets to release oppression and let truth shine.

DANCE OF THE SEVEN VEILS—BUT MAKE THAT FOURTEEN

The following exercise is a new version of an exploration I shared in my book *Walking in Beauty*. This dance is about releasing external expectations and labels and then putting on the things that you most desire.

Start this process by sitting down with your journal open to two blank pages. On the left blank page, write down all the things you are ready to release—names you have carried, titles you have earned and no longer want, descriptions that are hurtful or harmful—that you have taken into your spirit nonetheless. Write down the words and names you are ready to let go of.

On the right blank page, write down all the things you desire to be. These could be attributes, goals, titles, or successes. What do you want to embody?

Go back through each list and circle seven words to release and seven words to take in.

After you have your two lists, go and collect seven pieces of clothing that you have no personal attachment to. These should be clothes you are ready to get rid of, throw away, or donate. Name each of these pieces of clothing for one of the attributes you are ready to release. Set them aside.

Now go and collect seven pieces of clothing that make you feel beautiful, fabulous, or powerful. If you don't have any clothes that make you feel this way, pick out clothing items that are comfortable or neutral. Write out the seven attributes you are releasing on strips of paper and pin them to the corresponding clothes and set them aside.

The clothing you pick for this process can be anything. You don't need to go out and get new pieces of clothing. Jeans, fancy dresses, kilts, robes, long socks, top hats, veils, jackets, sneakers … Anything works.

Then write out the seven attributes you are calling in on strips of paper and pin them to the corresponding clothes. Spread these items around the room where you will be performing the ritual.

Put a mirror in the place where you will be performing the ritual.

Keep in mind that the dancing called for in this ritual can look any way. You don't need to be pulling off professional ballroom moves, or twerk, or do anything complicated. Dancing can look like sitting in a chair and moving your arms. Dancing can be tapping your feet or bobbing your head. Dancing can be wild and ecstatic for a few seconds and then a gentle swaying. Let dancing be whatever your body allows.

Set up a playlist of music that makes you want to dance. It can be music from any genre as long as it makes you want to move your body to it. Be sure the playlist is at least an hour long so you have plenty of time to be immersed in the magick of it.

Create a space where you have enough room to dance around. If you have to push the couch back or move a table into the corner, then do it. You want to be able to shake and move your body freely. If this type of space doesn't exist where you live, see if you can borrow a friend's place. Set up a full-length mirror in the space.

Start by taking a cleansing shower or bath. Do a salt scrub or make a tea out of sage, bay leaf, hyssop, and basil and add that tea water to your bath. When the bath is finished, turn on your music ...[22]

Put on only the clothes of the attributes you want to release. Don't put on any other clothing. As you put on each of these seven items, say the word you are releasing out loud. Feel the weight of these words pressing against you via the clothing.

Move your body and name one of the attributes you want to release. Feel it. This might be very difficult; you might want to scream or cry or yell. Follow your body's instincts. Do what feels necessary, but then take off that piece of clothing. Set it down, stomp on it, let it go, say goodbye to it. Leave that piece of clothing in a ball on the floor. It no longer matters. It's no longer yours.

Repeat this process with the six remaining items of clothing. When you are once again naked, look at yourself in the mirror and offer yourself a blessing. Speak from your heart. If words

---

22. LeFae, *Walking in Beauty*, 169.

elude you, say, "I am powerful and whole. I am a force to be reckoned with. I am divine!"

Let the music move you again, this time swirling around the room and picking up those other pieces of clothing with the attributes that you want to call in. Put on one garment and say the word out loud as you do so. Feel the power of that word seep into you, taking up the place of one of the words you just released. Feel it glow and charge within you. Dance with it. Let it soak into you.

Again, repeat this process. Pick up each item, feel it, sing to it, dance with it, and take it into yourself. When you have taken on all seven attributes and are wearing all seven items of clothing, stand in front of the mirror again and see yourself as a shining powerhouse of magick.

When you feel complete with this process, you can take off the seven veils of power. Read the new attributes you have taken on in front of the mirror. Then say, "I am this. I am this. I am this."

Walking while Dancing

I use the word *dancing* here to really mean movement. Movement and embodiment are very important processes in the world of the heretic. Spiritual seekers and world changers can spend a lot of time thinking. We can even spend a lot of time arguing and trying to get our points across to those who seem to be totally clueless—or worse, abusive.

But words and thoughts only go so far. Salome shows us that we need to feel the thing, move it into our bodies, and experience it on the physical level. There is no spiritual path or calling that will encourage you to just sit back and think. Meditation and emotional processing are important, but they are only pieces of the pie. Don't forget your body.

Salome understood her body. She understood what it did and what its power truly was. She grasps us by the hand and helps us connect with the same thing.

Do you hate your body? Are you uncomfortable in your skin? These are important things to change. Just keep in mind that the shift from discomfort to enjoyment doesn't happen overnight. It is a slow process that will come with peaks and valleys. Don't expect to go to bed one night and awaken the next morning in love with yourself.

But please, do the work to love your body. Salome would want you to. Ask your body what it needs. Find out how it best likes to move. Discover what foods are best for your particular metabolism. Rub lotion into your sore muscles. Find kindness in your heart for yourself and your body.

Salome danced her way into legend. We all can too.

༄ Traveling to the Realm of Salome ༄

Salome is available to show us the rhythm of our dancing. She connects us with the power of our bodies without having to leave our house. Lucky us! A visit with this heretical woman can help us connect back into our bodies and find the path to embodiment.

Supplies: A veil (or thin piece of fabric) and a glass-encased candle of any color you like.

Set Up: It is best to perform this working after the sun has set, but anytime will do. Set out something lovely to eat and drink for yourself after you have completed the ritual. Create a place where you can sit or lie down comfortably for an extended period of time without being disrupted.

When you are ready, light the candle, place the veil over your head, and say:

Salome, dance with me.
Salome, twirl with me.
Salome, move your hips and guide my heart.
Salome, Salome, I call to you.
Blessed be.

Trance: Let your physical body be as comfortable as possible. Breathe deeply, feeling the pulse and flow of air and blood move through you. Take a moment to scan your physical body and see how you are feeling. Do you need to adjust your position? Do you need a pillow or blanket? Make sure your physical needs are met. (Long pause.)

With each breath, allow your edges to soften a bit. Feel yourself become light and soft and wide and expansive. Allow your breathing to slow, each breath a prayer, each breath a deepening. (Pause.)

From this place of expansion and softness, allow your witch's eye to open. And as it does, you see before you a path. Take a step on this path, one foot in front of the other, following along. As you move, you can hear revelry in the distance. As you move closer to that noise, you see before you a bright and lavish outdoor party. (Pause.)

There is instrumental music and lush, cushioned fabrics spread out around a lantern-lit garden. There are the scents of perfume and spiced foods in the air. People are laughing and smiling and carrying on, enjoying the gathering.

From the depth of the crowded party, a young woman emerges. She is dressed in a dancer's garb and she moves with grace. It is Salome. She smiles broadly to you and gestures for you to follow her. She grasps your hand and pulls you deep into the throng of dancers and partygoers.

With her encouragement, you move, twirl, shift, and shimmy to the sound of the music and the drums. Salome dances with you, a grin on her face and sweat standing out on her brow. (Pause.)

The music begins to slow and you notice the partygoers are slowly disappearing, leaving you and Salome alone in this beautifully decorated celebration space. Take this moment to speak with her. Ask her the question you hold deep in your heart and hear what she has to say about the wisdom of your body. (Long pause.)

Salome blows her breath into a veil; it glows with love and body acceptance. She places this veil over your head and it melts into you. A warmth and understanding fills your body. Let yourself feel loved. (Pause.)

Your time in this place is limited. Although you can return to visit Salome at any time, for now you must prepare to leave. Say anything else that needs to be said and ask any last questions of Salome. (Long pause.)

When you are ready, say your goodbyes and turn and walk away, one foot in front of the other, leaving behind the empty party space and returning to the path that led you here. Step by step, you move closer to your body. As you walk, allow your witch's eye to close, returning to its normal state of being.

Take long, slow, deep breaths and feel the softness of your body again. Continue to notice your breathing and as you do, pull your edges back in. Notice the confines of your skin. Notice the boundaries of your physicality. Breathe slowly and call yourself back to yourself.

When you feel ready, tap your edges and place your hands on top of your head. Say your name out loud three times and slowly open your eyes.

Welcome back!

Gently pull the veil off your head and blow out the candle. Take a moment to write down anything interesting or important that may have come up. If you feel so called, put on some music and dance to embody the experience.

BEING A HERETIC WITH SALOME

It's heretical to love your body. You know why? Take a look at the mainstream. We are constantly being told how we need to look, what shape our bodies should be, etc. In life, people are bombarded with images that don't look like us.

Of course, it's immensely powerful to see yourself represented in the mainstream. It can make you feel like you aren't alone. However, sometimes that representation isn't there. And so, you must be the one that represents. Who better to represent you than you?

Loving yourself, loving your body, and connecting with it as a primal and vital force of life is heretical. Salome can help show us the way.

✦ ✦ ✦ **Heretic Contemplation** ✦ ✦ ✦

Where in your life do you feel connected with your body, like Salome? Where can you see yourself as her? Take out your journal and set a timer for five minutes. Write down how you feel about your body right now, in this moment. Continue writing until the timer goes off.

When time is up, read over what you have written. Circle five words that stand out. If they are positive words, write them on a separate list. If they are negative words, write their opposite word down on this list.

With these words, create a chant, mantra, or prayer for your body. Let this be one of love and gratitude. Put it in a place where you can see it and recite it out loud daily.

PART FOUR

BEING THE WARRIOR

CHAPTER 12
THE WARRIOR WOMEN

What images come up for you when thinking about warrior women? Video games may influence this concept, bringing forth images of little feminine bodies with giant boobs. In video games, warrior women are often scantily clad and have a big weapon and unrealistic hairdos. Or maybe the phrase *warrior woman* has you picturing a painted warrior covered in furs and screaming from the edge of a forest.

People love to think about warrior women as if they are some anomaly and didn't actually exist all throughout history—or that they were some rare and precious thing. Lots of cultures over the years have had warriors of every gender, but the history taught in school classrooms greatly diminishes this truth and makes it seem like warrior women are a rare occurrence.

One definition of *warrior* is a brave or experienced fighter. Your imagination may go to one place when you think of fighting; it might look like knights on horseback, Vikings running into the fray of battle, or lines of soldiers in matching uniforms, stepping in unison. There's gotta be more to it than just that, right?

Even the word *fighting* can bring up certain preconceived images. Fighting isn't just bare knuckles in an alley behind a bar, knives in a flurry, or guns being fired. People fight in millions of ways. We fight for what we believe in. We fight for justice. We fight for rights, health, safety, and equality. We fight for our families and loved ones. Fighting comes in many forms. So do warriors.

Warrior women are rebels only in the modern concept of the term. Because again, anything rebellious comes from outside the norm or status quo. Therefore, if the expectation of a warrior is a man, anything else is rebellious.

I can already hear some folks saying, "But Phoenix, there are lots of women who are part of the modern armed forces. Wouldn't they be warrior women, and isn't that mainstream?" First of all, in the United States women have only been permitted to serve in combat since 2015.[23] As I write this sentence, that was only five years ago. FIVE! Plus, we are talking about warrior women here, not soldiers. Yes, plenty of women who serve in the armed forces do it as a spiritual calling, but that's not true for all folks serving. And, all women in the military are working against sexist standards. So, in a very real sense, they are all rebels, fighting against the status quo and oppression. Yes, folks who serve in the military are putting their lives on the line, and they deserve our respect. With that being said, there are more warriors in the world than military badasses.

---

23. Moore, "Women in Combat."

Alicia Garza, Opal Tometi, and Patrisse Cullors are warrior women for starting Black Lives Matter. Marsha P. Johnson, a prominent figure of the Stonewall Riots, is a warrior woman. Gloria Steinem is a warrior woman for standing up for equality and women's rights. None of these women were combat trained or military experts. None of these women threw punches or fought in duels. They were—and are—women who knew the world needed change and did something about that. Rebels in the form of warriors.

We need to learn from these warrior women so that we can become warriors ourselves. Warrior women show us the way to fight oppression, shift power structures, and demand a different world. Truly, we are in desperate need of warriors right now.

THE SHIELD

The tool of the warrior is the shield, and I'll be up-front in saying that this is a tricky tool. Shields do a lot. They are a form of protection and they are also a weapon, a way to push back. *Shield* is a noun and a verb; we hold a shield and we shield someone.

I would love to live in a world where shields aren't needed, but I don't. Shields are a necessary part of life. And using shields for yourself and for others is a really important part of the warrior's path.

There is potential for trouble with shields. If we aren't careful, shields can become things we hide behind, even when it's not necessary. Shields can turn into walls and suddenly, we can find ourselves trapped by a structure of our own making.

I often think of the Knight of Pentacles from tarot when shields come up. He is a warrior and knows how to use the tool of the shield to protect himself. But he has become too accustomed to being behind that shield. Now he is a little frozen, stuck, and emotionally unavailable. He doesn't have the wisdom to know when it is safe to take the shield down, and he is in serious danger of his shield turning into a wall.

Best case scenario, a shield is used when it is needed and then it is taken down, set aside, and left waiting for the next time it needs to be taken out.

Those of us walking the rebel's path, those of us that desire to be witches and warriors, need to shield up when necessary for our own emotional (and occasionally physical) safety. Just by being out and about in the world, we tend to pick up negative energy. The more we step into our rebellious selves, the more projections will be sent our way. The more attention we get for our good work, the more haters we accumulate. Sadly, this is also part of the work of the rebel and warrior.

Creating a spiritual shield is necessary to help the path stay as smooth as possible.

◎◍ Creating Your Spiritual Shield ◍◎

Complete this exercise when you are ready to build your own spiritual shield. You will need about thirty minutes of undisturbed time to devote to this process.

Find a place where you can sit or lie down comfortably. Make sure that all your physical needs are addressed, and have a glass of water nearby that you can drink after completing the trance. You may also want to have a journal and pen handy to write down important notes afterward.

Trance: Breathe deeply and allow yourself to feel the edges of your body. Keep breathing with intention and be with your breath. (Long pause.)

When you are ready, begin to scan your body energetically. See if there are any threads of your attention that are elsewhere, pulling at your energy or distracting you. If there are, simply unhook your attention and reel these pieces of you back into your body.

Keep breathing. Scan your body a few more times to release anything that doesn't serve you in this moment. (Long pause.)

When you are ready, connect to the seat of your willpower. This is most often found in the center of the body or the solar plexus. Connect with this place in your body and notice how it feels in this moment. (Pause.)

Feel your connection to the earth, whether this is through your feet or your tailbone. Feel the thread of energy that connects you to the planet. Imagine the connection is like a straw and begin to draw earth energy up through that connection and into your body, focusing it right into the solar plexus energy center. (Pause.)

Keep calling up that energy and building up the power of your solar plexus until it is large and thrumming and potentially a little uncomfortable. When it reaches that level of intensity, project that energy out in front of your body, like a shield.

Use all of the earth energy you have called up, not your own reserves. Build that shield with the power and strength of the earth. Let that shield become solid. And as it does, notice the details of what it looks like. (Pause.)

What material is it made from? How is it designed or decorated? What color and shape is it? Allow your shield to become firm and solid, taking in any special details about how it looks. (Long pause.)

When your shield is firm and solid, duplicate it and place the second shield behind you, protecting your back. Now feel your shields covering your front and back. Feel how strong and solid they are, connected to the earth. (Pause.)

Take a moment to practice calling these shields into your body and then popping them back out. Do this a few times, calling them in and then popping them back out. (Long pause.)

When you feel ready, call your shields into your body and shift your awareness to the edges of your body and your breathing. Pay attention to your breath, in and out. Use your hands to tap the edges of your body and then place your hands on the top of your head. When you feel ready, slowly open your eyes and take in your space.

Welcome back!

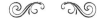

Drink the glass of water. Write any details about your shields in your journal. You may even want to draw the shields and add a little color.

> **✦ ✦ ✦ Personal Contemplation ✦ ✦ ✦**
>
> Do you feel like a warrior? Are there places in your life where you speak up, stand up, and fight for improvement? How do you imagine being a warrior would change your life?
>
> Take out your journal and write the word WARRIOR across the top of the page. Set a timer for five minutes and free write on this word. Everything and anything that comes up is fair game.
>
> When the timer goes off, set your journal aside for at least one full day. When you feel ready, read over what you've written. How does it make you feel?
>
> Then write the words I AM A WARRIOR on the top of a new page. Set a timer for five minutes and free write on what comes up for you with this statement.
>
> When the timer goes off, set your journal aside for at least one full day. When you are ready, read over what you've written. How does all of it make you feel? Are you ready to call yourself a warrior?

WARRIORS OF THIS BOOK

The warrior women you are about to meet stood up to injustice. They fought against oppression and did their part in creating a better world. They put their own lives at risk to lead rebellions and shift the power structures. We can learn from them; we can follow in their footsteps.

In the following chapters, we will explore the lives of three famous warrior women: Boudicca, Moving Robe Woman, and Harriet Tubman. You will have a chance to learn more about each of them, connect with their powers, and take one more step on your path to being a warrior.

With that, let's be on our way…

CHAPTER 13
BOUDICCA

All the women in this book fill me with awe, wonder, and pride. And yet, there is something about Boudicca (pronounced boo-di-kuh) that does that doubly so. I don't know why, but this legend has loomed large in my life for a very long time. Her story isn't an easy one to read.

Boudicca and her husband were the leaders of their tribe, the Iceni, in what is now called the United Kingdom. This was during the time of Roman occupation, right around 61 CE, and Boudicca would have been considered a Celt. For the most part, her tribe did their best to live amicably with the Romans, but after her husband died, all of that changed.

Boudicca is a bit of a mystery. We know almost nothing of her history before her interaction with Rome because the only records of her come from Roman record keeping. The Romans didn't give a hoot about anyone unless they caused them trouble or got in their way. Roman historian Cassius Dio leaves us with one of the only physical descriptions of Boudicca. He wrote she was very tall with hip-length yellowish hair, piercing eyes, and a harsh voice. She wore multicolored dresses with a gold torque and a thick cloak pinned with a brooch.[24] We don't know if Boudicca was originally from the Iceni tribe or if she was married in as a "noble" woman. We don't really know what her early life was like or anything about her potential training as a warrior before this moment.

When Boudicca wouldn't kowtow to the Romans, they publicly whipped her and sexually assaulted her two daughters. This disgusting and despicable act inflamed a warrior's passion in Boudicca's heart. She was done with the Romans, she was done with their occupation, she was done with their abuse, and she was even done with her own people, who were so willing to give in to the Roman's way of life.

The Roman occupiers had no idea Boudicca would react to what was done to her. The Roman powers-that-be expected her to just take the abuse because that is what people did under the heel of the Roman empire. But Boudicca was different. What Boudicca had on her side was surprise. She rallied her people, her own tribe, and they started to fight back. Her rebellion started in the year 61 CE and lasted for about a year.

A warband left her village with Boudicca leading the party. The Celts were known to be aggressive against Rome. They took their relationships with their kin and warriors-in-arms very seriously, watching each other's backs and treating each other like family. However fearsome, skilled, and tight-knit the Celts were, their numbers were nothing in comparison to the legions of Rome. I'm sure you've heard similar tales before.

Under Boudicca's leadership, the Iceni warriors and many others they gathered along their way demolished the city of Camulodunum (now known as Colchester in the United King-

---

24. Fields, *Boudicca's Rebellion AD 60–61*, 50.

dom. Boudicca and her warriors locked people—both Romans and Roman sympathizers—in the temple and burned the city to nothing. Her fury raged as the towns she sieged burned. Literally nothing was left in their wake except smoking piles of rubbish.

After the success at this location, Boudicca and her rebels set their sights on London, called Londinium at the time. The rebels found success and leveled the growing city. They then moved northward toward a small town called Verulamium and, again, left the town in ruins. These major losses were highly problematic for the Roman leadership in Britannia because the ruling emperor was very close to pulling Rome completely out of the region.

After Boudicca's rebels won Verulamium, the bulk of the Roman legions who had been fighting on the other side of the island started to make their way toward them. Where they met up is the site of Boudicca's last battle, although the specific location has been lost to time.

Up until this moment, Boudicca and her followers had not really fought in a true battle. They had taken towns, sure, but for the most part, these places were not well guarded and were mostly filled with average Roman citizens. In some cases, the towns were essentially deserted because the people knew they were under attack and escaped beforehand. A true battle against Roman soldiers was something else entirely.

Before this battle started, Boudicca rode in her chariot down the line of warriors with her two daughters next to her. She is quoted by Tacitus as saying, "Win this battle or perish. That is what I, a woman, plan to do—let the men live in slavery if they will."[25]

---

25. Fields, *Boudicca's Rebellion AD 60–61*, 75.

The Roman legions won that day. We don't know how things ended for Boudicca. All we know is that her body was not found and she was not captured by the Romans. Some believe Boudicca took her own life, but that doesn't seem plausible to me. Others believe that she was seriously wounded and died shortly thereafter, pulled away from the fray by her daughters or her warrior kin. We may never know the truth of the end of her life, but her legacy lives on.

Boudicca has become a symbol of fighting against oppression. Her story is well-known in the UK and she is remembered fondly, so much so that there is a huge statue of her in London, the same town she demolished. For many, Boudicca represents the ancient indigenous spirit of the land. She is a powerful symbol of sovereignty.

No matter where you are from or your ancestry, Boudicca can show you how to stand up for your own sovereignty. *Sovereignty* is the right of power to govern oneself. This word is often used to describe countries that are in negotiation or war with other countries. In Boudicca's time, sovereignty was also about relationship with the land and the rights of the land as a living entity. And I'm going to take it one step further: Boudicca helps us connect to our own personal sovereignty as a human individual.

There is little doubt Boudicca had a distaste for the Roman occupation, but she may have settled for a much quieter rebellion if her rights as a ruler weren't questioned and her children weren't abused. In modern day, it is easy for us to complain or defend our personal rights and the rights of our loved ones on social media. It's a whole other situation to ride a chariot into the middle of the battlefield and scream for justice.

Of Sovereignty and Chariots

The land is important. The longer a family lives in one area, the deeper their connection to that land becomes. Having a relationship with the land and working with the land as an ally is a big part of sovereignty. The whole concept of sovereignty is something that those of us born in North America don't really have a deep understanding of because our ancestry isn't from the land we live on. Personally, I find this terribly problematic and sad. This is one place where Boudicca can be a powerful teacher.

The actionable lesson from Boudicca comes in the form of the chariot. The Celts used chariots in battle in ways that were totally new and revolutionary to the Roman legions. Boudicca herself charged into battle on a chariot, her two young daughters with her.

Chariots are symbols of action, movement, and success. The magick of Boudicca is one of success and seeing your goals manifest. The connection to the chariot gives you forward momentum. Just make sure you know where you are going—you're gonna get there fast!

Sovereignty

The actual definition of *sovereignty* is supreme power and authority. In order to live in balance with the world and with each other, it would behoove us to say that the only thing in this world that has supreme power and authority is the land itself.

I'm not referring to the land in regard to resources or anything super mundane like that. I mean this more as the sovereignty of the land, speaking of the land as if it is its own sovereign being. Because it is.

This is big. It isn't just about you, your future, or even your family's future. It's a bigger level consideration. Honoring the sovereignty of the land means you make major decisions based on how they might impact the generations down the line.

Warriors understand how important this is. Warriors rarely fight for or make decisions based on their own needs as an individual. Warriors fight for something bigger than themselves. This can be seen from people who are involved in social justice work all the way to people who enlist in the military. These folks see a cause—something bigger than themselves—that they want to support, help, fix, or fight for, and they put themselves on the line to create change.

If you were to picture life seven generations from now, what would you hope the world looked like? Would you hope for more peace and cooperation? Would you hope for more equality? Would you hope for a healthy planet that supports your descendants? I know that I do. These are things that call to my rebel heart. These are the things that fire me up and inspire me to fight.

From a place of personal autonomy, who has supreme power and authority over you? The answer to that is simple: You do. So many of us give our personal sovereignty away all the time. We say yes when we really mean no. We put another person's needs ahead of our own. We promise our time and energy out of obligation and not out of desire.

What would it be like if you only said yes out of desire?

What would it be like if you only said yes to things that you felt excited about or called to?

What would it be like if you waited to receive a clear yes from your own self before taking on a project, commitment, or agreement?

"But Phoenix, I've got kids and parents to take care of. I've got responsibilities. I gotta bring in the bucks. Sometimes I have to do things." I hear you. Life is life, and we all have responsibilities that we might not feel a strong desire to fulfill. I know this. I get this. Not only do I run a business, but I have kids, parents, a sister, a spouse, in-laws, a dog, and a cat. I have commitments and a house to take care of. And sometimes I have to do things that I don't want to, like clean the house.

However, I agreed to all these commitments with a strong yes within myself. I agreed to the pets I have, therefore, my ongoing responsibility is to care for them. I agreed to be the best parent I can be even on my bad days. I have chosen to have a relationship with my parents and sister. I picked my spouse. And I chose my business. These are all things I said a resounding yes to. Those yeses can change, of course, but then it would be my responsibility to sever that relationship, make changes, or do something different. It might not be easy, but it is ultimately my responsibility.

Big life commitments, although important, are only a part of the picture. This concept also includes the small daily agreements we make. The times we say yes when we want to say no. These are moments when we ignore our personal sovereignty. They add up and end up hurting us in the long run.

This could look like having sex because the other person wants to. Or making cookies for the school bake sale because the other parents are bringing something. Or agreeing to take on a project because no one else is stepping up to volunteer. Often, we say yes to things out of obligation when we want to say no. Rather than going to sleep early because we are tired, we end up having sex. Rather than taking that relaxing bath, we bake those cookies. Rather than going to the beach for a day of rejuvenation, we do all the groundwork for a project we don't care about.

These small things, these small capitulations, eat away at our personal sovereignty.

> ### ✦ ✦ ✦ Personal Contemplation ✦ ✦ ✦
>
> Where do you give your personal sovereignty away? For the next week, track all the things you are asked to do. Before saying yes to anything, pause and check in with yourself. Is this something you really want to do? Is this something you have the capacity to hold? Are you committing because you want to, or is it because you feel obligated?
>
> Try this for one week and then explore your results. Can you try it for a second week?

Chariots

It is well documented that the Celts used chariots as part of their battle plan, and Boudicca is remembered leading her rabble of fighters from a chariot pulled by two horses. The Romans were so enamored with the chariot's potential for fighting that they often wrote about it in their records and attempted to use this tactic in their own fighting.

The tool of Boudicca the warrior woman is the chariot. How do you get from here to there? How do you lead an army? How does your voice reach as many people as possible? Why, from a chariot of course!

The Chariot in tarot is one of the cards of the major arcana. It is a trump card and it carries a lot of weight. The tarot is almost like two decks of cards in one; the minor arcana is like a regular deck of playing cards, while the major arcana are all the trumps. The messages of the major arcana are deeper and bolder, and they can shift the energy of a reading because of their influence. When

I do readings for clients and the Chariot makes an appearance, I always take it as a positive omen.

In tarot, the Chariot is a card of success and action. It tells the story of moving forward. It is a card of encouragement for you to go after what you desire because you will find success. This is a card of channeling your fierce power toward your most outlandish goals.

CHARIOT SYMBOLS OF SUCCESS

One of my favorite ways of working with tarot is using specific cards as touchstones. As you step deeper into the life of a rebel, you may need visual reminders of your badassery. If you need a reminder of your rebellious nature, or if you need something to meditate with to connect to your rebel or warrior power, the Chariot is a great ally for that.

If you've got a tarot deck, pull out the Chariot card and place it on your bathroom mirror or another place you will see it regularly. If you don't have a tarot deck, look up artwork online where independent artists are selling their work. You are likely to find lots of options for your own Chariot card.

When you see this card, let it be a reminder that you are fierce and you will achieve your dreams.

WALKING WHILE FIGHTING

I'm going to admit something to you: The hardest part of being a warrior woman is the potential for burnout. Being a warrior requires a level of output and energy. I don't know about you, but even the word *fight* makes me feel a little bit tired. I don't have a lot of energy to expend with all my regular life stuff. Putting out even more energy is just a lot to carry.

Self-care is imperative to being a witch, heretic, and warrior. However, self-care has become a bit of a buzzword. There are self-care social media accounts with photos of beautiful bathtubs filled with rose petals, robed women getting massages, and sweet, sweet pampering. That's not self-care—not completely.

Self-care is knowing your limits and not getting to the point of burnout. Self-care is saying no to obligations when there is already too much on your plate. Self-care is pacing yourself. Self-care is delegating. Self-care is taking breaks, eating regularly, bathing regularly, and getting outside as often as possible.

Boudicca fought until the very last moment, but she knew she was burning the candle from both ends. She knew she was fighting a battle that would end in her death. Modern witches, heretics, and warriors can make better choices. We can take care of ourselves as an act of rebellion.

You don't have to work yourself to the point of exhaustion to prove your value. You don't have to keep going when the tank is empty or seek external validation. You only need to take care of you. That is fighting the good fight from a modern perspective.

And again, I find myself hearing the voices of readers who are saying, "How is this witchcraft?" All I can say to that is: It is. Self-care is revolutionary in a world that wants us to go-go-go. It is magick that empowers and enlivens us. Remember, know thyself. You can only discover who you are when you take the time to care for yourself.

❧ Traveling to the Realm of Boudicca ❧

You don't have to cover your body with woad, carry a spear, and scream while running down a hill to connect with Boudicca, the warrior queen. However, if you really want to, I highly recommend it.

Supplies: An image of Boudicca that you love, a ceremonial weapon (like an athame, a special knife, or a sword), and your favorite incense.

Set Up: Put the image of Boudicca in the center of your working area and place the ceremonial weapon near it. Light the incense and sit in contemplation of what it means to be a warrior in your life. If possible, sit up as straight as possible with your feet flat on the floor.

Trance: Take a deep breath and feel the beating of your heart. Even if you can't physically feel the pulse, pretend that you can. Feel the gentle tapping of the heartbeat rhythm of your body. Breathe in and out, slowly and deliberately. Feel the beating of your heart matched by the beating of the earth's heart below you. Sit in this place of connection. (Pause.)

As you breathe, let your edges soften. Allow the barriers that hold you to open and expand, shifting your awareness. Let yourself get wider, bigger, and softer. Expand. (Pause.)

As you continue to expand, allow your witch's eye to open. When that eye is open, you see in front of you a path that winds into an oak forest. Take a few steps along this path and step into the deep cover of the forest trees. With one foot in front of the other, move along the path, taking note of any plant or animal allies that may show up along the way. (Pause.)

Hear the crunch of leaves under your feet and the scent of wet earth as you walk along this path. Suddenly, you reach an opening in the trees and a meadow opens up in front of you. You can hear a noise in the distance, a rattling and the stamping of horses' hooves. The sound gets louder and louder, coming ever closer to the meadow.

On the other side of the meadow, Boudicca comes bursting out from the trees on a Celtic chariot pulled by two small but strong horses. She circles around the meadow, whooping and hollering. She comes to a stop and gestures for you to approach.

When you are ready, go up to the chariot and speak with Boudicca. Ask her whatever questions you have about your own warrior path and your personal sovereignty, and see what answers wait for you. (Long pause.)

After a while, Boudicca takes you into her chariot and clicks her tongue, encouraging the horses to start moving. They begin to walk, pulling the chariot at a slow and gentle pace. She clicks her tongue again, and the horses pick up speed a bit. Boudicca steers the chariot in a circle around the meadow, moving more quickly. Feel the exhilaration as the wind brushes over you. Allow the power of the rumbling chariot, horses' hooves, and wind to energize your warrior's heart. (Pause.)

Boudicca whistles and the horses quickly come to a stop. She helps you get down from the chariot. Take some time now to say anything else in your heart and to hear the final bits of Boudicca's wisdom. (Long pause.)

The time has come to leave this place for now, although you can return here at any time. Offer your thanks and gratitude to Boudicca. When you feel ready, find your way back to the path that brought you here. You step back into the cover of the trees and continue walking the path back home.

As you walk the path, allow your witch's eye to return to its normal state of being. And as that eye closes, feel again the confines of your body. Notice your breath and connect to your body. Allow the pieces of you that expanded to close up, coming back into your body with each breath you take.

Tap the edges of your body with your hands. Let your awareness focus on your earlobes, your shoulders, your toes. Breathe deeply and place your hands on the top of your head. Speak your name out loud three times. And when you feel ready, slowly open your eyes.

Gently stretch your body, feeling how your body wants to move and allowing it to do so.

Welcome back!

Take some time to write down anything interesting or important about the journey that you would like to remember.

BEING A WARRIOR WITH BOUDICCA

Boudicca saw the injustice happening to the people around her for most of her life. She saw the impact of oppression on her people. However, when that injustice arrived at her own door—when the Romans assaulted Boudicca and her children—that was the straw that broke the camel's back. That was when she became the warrior who jumped into the chariot to demand change.

There are times in our lives where we look at personal situations, community situations, or global situations and have to say "Enough!" Boudicca, Queen of the Iceni, thorn in Rome's side, knows all about it. She can help us find the revolution needed in our own lives. It doesn't matter if that revolution is to change a relationship, a work situation, a community problem, or a global issue. Revolution is here. The time for change is well overdue.

With Boudicca's help, we can learn how to fight for the lives we want, set better boundaries, and live with courage and confidence. Are you ready, warrior?

✦ ✦ ✦ **Warrior Contemplation** ✦ ✦ ✦

Where in your life can you see yourself honoring your sovereignty like Boudicca? Where in your life is it time for a revolution? Take some time to write about the places in your life that aren't working, need an upgrade, could use change, or are just downright broken. Even if your life is perfectly amazing, there is still likely to be something you'd like to improve or change.

What is one thing you can do right now to start making that situation better?

CHAPTER 14
MOVING ROBE WOMAN

Have you ever heard of Moving Robe Woman? I'm guessing most people haven't. She is one of the greatest North American heroes there has ever been. Moving Robe Woman, whose name in her native language is Tȟašína Máni, was also known as Her Eagle Robe and Mary Crawler. She was a member of the Hunkpapa Sioux Tribe during the mid-1800s to early 1900s.

Moving Robe Woman was born in 1854, but very little is known about her life before her early twenties. We know stories of her as a young woman because she was one of the warriors who fought against Custer and his men at the Battle of Little Big Horn.

Here are some things we do know. We know her mother's name was Sunflower Face. Her father, who was leader of her tribe's warband, was called Slohan or Crawler. We know she had at least one brother called Deeds, who was also known as One Hawk.

We also know that Moving Robe Woman lived into her early 80s and died in her own log cabin on the Standing Rock Reservation in South Dakota. She had a couple dozen horses and cattle at the time of her passing. Her early life is totally a mystery. Her later life is totally a mystery. But there is one short stretch of time that we have major details about.

There are a lot of assumptions that can be made about Moving Robe Woman's life because of her status as a Sioux woman. Her late teens and early twenties were spent fighting against the oppression of the American government, and even after some of those troubles were "settled," life didn't get easier or better for the indigenous peoples of North America.

In an interview Moving Robe Woman did with Frank B. Zahn in 1931, she shared she had fought with a Sioux war band against the Crow tribe when she was just seventeen years old.[26] Although still young during the Battle of Little Big Horn, she was already an experienced fighter by the age of twenty-three. It's likely she was trained as a warrior since early on in life because her father was the war chief of the tribe. We know many Native American tribes had women warriors. It wasn't that much of a rarity. But the warriors of these tribes were familiar with a very different kind of warfare than what the American settlers brought with them. Moving Robe Woman's story is one of loss and grief. In fact, it was grief that propelled her into joining the final battle with Custer in the first place.

In the Battle of Little Big Horn, also known as Custer's Last Stand, Moving Robe Woman was one of the warriors who fought for liberation. When the fighting broke out, she was digging for turnips with the other young women. Riders came through the encampments, shouting that soldiers were coming. Women, children, and older men started to make their way to the hills, where it should have been safe from any fighting. Moving Robe Woman

---

26. Hardorff, *Lakota Recollections of the Custer Fight*, 90–96.

ran to her own tipi as her father readied their horses. It was at that moment she was struck with grief; Inside the tipi, her mother told her that her brother had been murdered by the soldiers.

In my imagination, I can feel this moment. I can see how the world likely slowed down for her, as if things were happening in slow motion. I can feel my heart beat as hers must have been upon receiving such terrible news. I can see the movement of horses and humans as bullets started to be fired into the camp. I can hear the echoing sounds of a warrior shouting to the others to charge.

After experiencing such hardship and trauma for so much of her life, this moment was more than her heart could bear.

Moving Robe Woman's heart was broken and she could only think about the life of her younger brother that had been taken away. She wanted revenge. She wanted to make the people who had killed him pay for that crime. "I ran to a nearby thicket and got my black horse. I painted my face with crimson and braided my black hair. I was mourning. I was a woman, but I was not afraid."[27]

Women and children ran for cover from the bullets of the soldier's guns. While they were running away, Moving Robe Woman jumped on her horse and rode for the soldiers and the front line. Over the sounds of battle, she could hear the older men and women singing the death songs for the warriors facing battle, which were meant to give the warrior strength and bravery as they faced death. Hearing their voices made her feel brave. She rode into battle with her father at her side.

Accounts of this (in)famous battle have been written about and written about. The accounts of soldiers and the American

---

27. Hardorff, *Lakota Recollections of the Custer Fight*, 93.

government tell one story and the Sioux warriors tell another. Suffice it to say the soldiers' accounts speak in highly negative— and of course, unprovable—ways about the actions of the Sioux warriors. And although Sitting Bull and the Sioux won the Battle of Little Big Horn, many of the Sioux who fought were later tracked down and killed. They were killed at the hands of Custer's soldiers or through illness and poor care while in governmental custody.

There is one witness of the battle who said Moving Robe Woman stabbed Custer in the chest during the battle. However, official reports don't say anything about Custer having stab wounds. And Moving Robe Woman never spoke publicly about killing him, not that I would blame her for keeping that bit of information to herself.

The day after the battle, Moving Robe Woman and many of the remaining members of the tribe moved north to Canada. She stayed there for many years before returning to the Standing Rock Reservation.

Moving Robe Woman died in 1935. There is little to no information about family that may have been with her or if she went on to have children, but her legend lives on.

Of Grief and Horses

Witches, heretics, and warrior women will face grief. I mean, grief is simply a part of life. However, in my experience, a rebel's relationship with grief is often more intense, aware, and alive. Heretics see what is broken and want to stand up to fix it. When you pay attention to injustice and the troubles in the world, it opens you up to be more connected to your empathy.

What this really means is you feel for others. Therefore, heretics must have a relationship with their grief and know how to work with it and through it. Seeing injustice is painful. Feeling injustice is traumatizing.

And yes, there is more to being a warrior than fighting and fear. Moving Robe Woman also helps us to reconnect with our animal allies. She speaks in her interview about her black horse. There is a special relationship between humans and horses, and this relationship goes back thousands of years. Warriors must have a solid relationship with all their allies, including animals.

Grief

When you, as a heretic, pay attention to injustice and decide that you want to do something about that injustice, this impacts you twofold.

The thing is when you start to see where things are out of balance and where people are treated wrongly, this will also point to things that aren't quite in balance internally as well. Remember the phrase "know thyself"? Well, here it is again. It's hard to look outside of yourself and see problems without starting to see where some of those same issues may be happening in your internal landscape. Seeing these injustices both internally and externally can bring up grief.

Empathy helps us feel the suffering of others. Is this fun? Hell no! But it *is* important. We don't want others to suffer, do we? No. And yet, suffering is happening all the time. As I am writing these words, people are suffering all over the world. That breaks my heart. I can't solve or stop any of that, but I can be aware.

And then I can look at where I have allowed injustice in my own life. How I have let other people have power over me. How I have given away my sovereignty. How I have punished myself or been cruel to myself. Seeing the places where I have allowed myself to be treated poorly, by others or by myself, is also a grief-creating awareness.

It is painful to see how you may have thwarted your own success. It brings real grief to think of the times you have wasted opportunities by keeping yourself small. Warriors don't allow for that to happen to other people. That is exactly what they are fighting for! But for a moment, us modern warriors need to look internally.

⟨⟩ Ritual for the Road Not Taken ⟨⟩

Occasionally, I look back on the road not taken. I allow myself to wander down the paths I didn't follow or left behind. Of course, it's all fantasy to walk these roads. But what would my life look like if I had finished college? What would my world be like if I had never divorced my daughter's father? How might life look if I had never left the corporate world? Some of these roads are fun and silly to walk down and imagine what could be, while others are a bit painful, bringing up regret and lost potential. It's these that we are going to focus on now.

Before performing this ritual, give yourself plenty of time to walk down the paths of those choices you didn't take. Do this through meditation, journaling, daydreaming, or walking and letting your mind wander; whatever works best for you. This could take some time. Ask yourself the question "What if?" and see where it goes.

If you find yourself hitting a point of sadness, loss, or regret, this is where the power is. That power is locked up and trapped in that choice. If you can unravel the stuck energy, you can take it back. This will feed you now and give you more power and energy.

Many of us leave bits of our power behind in the past. When we experience trauma, loss, or even a moment of any kind of heightened emotion, there is a chance we will fracture our energy. Most often we immediately take that power back; we do it without even thinking. But occasionally that fracture is permanent and you leave a piece of yourself behind in that moment or in that place. Some of the moments where we made specific choices, where we took one path and left another behind, create these fractures. This type of fracturing isn't actually permanent, but you have to consciously take those pieces of yourself back.

For this ritual I do not recommend going to the most painful or triggering experience, memory, or choice from the past. In fact, I don't recommend doing that on your own at any point. If you want to reengage fractured parts of yourself from major trauma, it is best to do that work with a trained soul retrieval practitioner or licensed therapist. If you attempt this process on your own, it could lead to further trauma.

For the purposes of this ritual, pick a memory or path where you have some wounding, but not trauma.

Supplies: A large bowl of water, a small bowl of water, a small bowl of salt, paper, an ink pen, a white glass-encased candle, and several sticks or cones of incense to burn for cleansing (like sage, frankincense, or dragon's blood).

Set Up: It is best if you perform this ritual outdoors, but if that isn't possible, make sure you can be in a space where there is an open window. A new moon is the best time to perform this ritual. Create a small, simple altar with all the items arranged in a pleasing way for you.

Take a moment to center yourself and bring yourself fully present for the ritual. You can do this by taking some deep cleansing breaths or clearing away any distraction, sitting or standing with your spine elongated and your focus on the items on your altar.

When you feel ready, light the white candle as a reminder of your divine spark. Take a moment to connect with the candle flame and let that flame remind you that you are a divine being. Feel your own inner flame as a twin to the candle.

Light one of the pieces of incense and watch the smoke as it rises up. Allow this to connect you to your allies and guides. Your will, messages, and desires are heard and supported by unseen allies who want nothing more than for you to find comfort and peace in your life. Take a moment to feel that connection. If you feel so called, speak your gratitude to them.

When you feel ready, refer back to the paths not taken. Using pen and paper, write out one of these paths. You can write just one sentence of the path's possibilities or allow yourself to fully go down that road and write down all the potential from that path.

During this process, you may be overcome with emotion. Let yourself feel and express what comes through. If there is grief and sadness, let yourself cry. If there is joy or bittersweet memories, laugh. If there is anger, let yourself rage. Feel the emotions.

You may also need to do more than just cry or laugh through this process. You may need to move your body and get it out physically. You may need to paint or draw to move these feelings. You may need to drum or sing. Let yourself express these emotions as much as you need to and in whatever way feels appropriate. Let this take the time that it needs.

When you are ready, drop the pages that you have written into the large bowl of water. Watch as the ink begins to smudge and smear and loosen.

Take a moment to meditate, visualize, or think about this choice, this moment. See yourself standing at a crossroads. See the path that you didn't take and the path that you did. Let yourself experience peace for the choices you have made.

As you visualize or imagine this, notice a small bit of yourself that has been left at this crossroads. Maybe it's a bit of glowing light. Maybe it is a bit of fabric. Maybe it's color or energy or something else. But see this bit of you that you have been living without and call it home. Pick it up, breathe it in, and reabsorb it. It will feel like clicking a puzzle piece into place or the ability to take a deeper breath.

When this process feels complete, let go of the visualization and return your focus to the paper soaking in the large bowl of water. Notice how the ink has been further loosened by the water.

Now pour the salt into the second small bowl of water and stir it with the fingers of your dominant hand. As you stir, say, "I release this path and I call myself back."

Sprinkle yourself with the salted water. Dip your fingers into the water and rub it on the back of your neck, your third eye, your heart, and your solar plexus. Rub the water into the palms of your hands and the soles of your feet.

If you feel emotions coming through as you do this, allow them to come on fully and express them as needed. Take the time that you need to feel complete in this process.

Set the salted water down and light several incenses at once so you have a nice amount of smoke. Carefully use the incense to smoke cleanse yourself. Swirl the incense around your body, focusing on any areas your intuition calls for. Remember the back of your neck, the palms of your hands, your feet, your heart, and the place where your legs join.

As you move the smoke over your body, say, "I am whole and complete. I call myself back." Take as much time as you need with the smoke cleanse.

When you feel ready, set down the incense and shift your focus to the candle. Feel your own divine essence glowing as the candle glows. Imagine the flame of the candle glowing in your heart mirrored by the candle flame in front of you. Let yourself be lit from the inside by this glow, this glowing of your divine self. Allow that flame to expand and grow, enveloping your entire body. You are a glowing, divine being.

Sit in this awareness for as long as you want or need to. You are a glowing, divine being.

When you feel ready, snuff out the candle and incense. Pour the salted water down the drain or flush it down the toilet.

At dawn the next morning, take the water-soaked paper to a crossroads and pour it out, releasing it.

Repeat this process for any other untaken paths that you are ready to release whenever you feel ready to release them.

Horses

Moving Robe Woman spoke about her black horse in her interview. The relationship between warrior and horse is a bond that is rarely seen in other situations. Warriors and their horses become one life, one bonded unit—not a human, not a horse, but something greater.

Animal allies are an important relationship for any heretic to have. Much like the plant allies we discussed in chapter 9, animal allies help reveal where we are blocked, where we need to make changes, and what energies we may want to call in to help us improve.

I'm often asked by students and clients, "How do you know when an animal is your ally?" The answer to this question is actually a lot simpler than it might seem.

Have you heard the sentiment about a reason, a season, or a lifetime? This is often used to describe human relationships, but it also applies to any kind of ally.

Sometimes an animal ally comes into our lives just for one reason, to teach us one lesson or highlight one moment. Sometimes they come into our lives for a season, where we spend a significant amount of time with them and there are many lessons learned. Others come into our lives for a lifetime and we learn lessons on the regular. It might feel like they have always been a part of our lives.

An animal ally might introduce itself to you by revealing itself in an unexpected way, like seeing a wild animal in a place you've never seen one before or having an interaction with a wild animal that seems special or otherworldly. This has the potential for an animal ally situation.

You might also feel connected to an animal. Maybe you really love horses, pigs, wolves, elephants, or some other animal. You collect images of them, know everything about them, and have a soul bond with them. This has the potential for an animal ally situation.

And then there are those animal allies who we invite into our lives. The cats, dogs, birds, fish, lizards, amphibians, and so on who become members of our families. They might not speak the same language that humans do, but we understand each other.

The good news is, you don't have to pick just one animal ally. There are lots of animals you might work with on a spiritual level.

⟲ Finding Your Animal Ally ⟳

You might already have a good idea about an animal ally or two, but the following trance exercise will help to bring out the animal ally that you should attempt to work with right now.

Sit or lie down as comfortably as possible. Make sure you can be undisturbed for at least thirty minutes.

Trance: Take several slow, deep breaths. Allow yourself to relax and soften. Let each inhale soften your edges and relax you more deeply. Let each exhale soften your edges and relax you more deeply. (Pause.)

As you breathe, open your witch's eye. With that eye open, you see before you a path. Start taking one step and then another, following along this path. Take note of where you are and what is around you. See if there are any specific sights or sounds that come through as you walk the path. Take note of the landscape, the time of day, and any other important details as you follow the path step by step.

As you walk along, you find yourself in a clearing or opening in the landscape. Let yourself wander in this space, in this opening. Take some time to explore. (Pause.)

Suddenly, you hear a noise from the other side of the clearing. A creature emerges. It might fly or crawl, it might float as if swimming in invisible water, or it might walk or run. It comes toward you. (Pause.)

Take in everything there is to see with this creature. You might want to try and speak to it and see if it answers you, whether with language or something else. (Long pause.)

When you feel ready, offer a moment of gratitude to the creature that has shown up for you today. Say thank you and watch as your ally disappears.

Find your way back to the path that brought you to this clearing. Follow the path, one foot in front of the other. As you walk forward on the path, feel that witch's eye close back down into its normal state.

Shift your awareness back into your body. With each inhale and exhale, notice the boundaries of your body get more and more firm. Place your hands on your solar plexus and take a deep breath. Place your hands on the top of your head and take a deep breath.

Slowly open your eyes and look around the space.

Welcome back!

Write down anything interesting, odd, or important that may have happened during your journey. Drink a glass of water.

Take some time to research the animal that visited you. Learn about how they live, what they eat, and their life cycles. These details will provide you with important bits of information for your own path. Pay attention to other ways this ally may show up in your life.

Walking while Broken

There are moments in life when we are broken, when we don't know if we can keep going. We see a moment like this in the story of Moving Robe Woman. When she learns of the death of her brother, she is hit with a grief like nothing she had experienced before. And in that moment, she had choices.

She could have run away and hid. She could have fallen to pieces and collapsed in a puddle on the ground. But she didn't do either of these things. She used her grief to fight back and try to prevent what happened to her brother from happening to anyone else.

When we are hit with harsh circumstances, we have choices. We can collapse or we can fight our way forward. Neither choice is wrong. Sometimes we must collapse first in order to be ready to keep moving forward.

Traveling to the Realm of Moving Robe Woman

The best person to train a warrior is another warrior. Only someone who has been through battles will really be able to understand what it takes to prepare another warrior for the fight. We can visit with Moving Robe Woman to learn what we need to do in our own lives to become a better warrior. We will meet her at a point in time many years after the Battle of Little Big Horn.

Supplies: A glass of water and a scattering of tobacco leaves as an offering.

Set Up: Find a place where you can be comfortable and lie down or sit as comfortably as possible. Set the glass of water next to you. If you are performing this ritual outdoors, sprinkle the tobacco on the ground in front of you. If you are performing this ritual indoors, burn a small bit of the tobacco.

Trance: Take a slow, deep breath. As you inhale, feel the air fill up your entire body. Hold your breath for a count of two and then give yourself a long, slow exhale. Repeat this process with a long, slow inhale and a long, slow exhale. Let this deep breathing begin to expand your awareness and shift your energy. With each inhale and exhale, you become more and more open. (Pause.)

Expand and grow wider and bigger. Let the edges of your body be soft and open. As your energy opens, also open your witch's eye.

See before you a path. All around you are wide open, rolling hills. They are green and lush, and you can hear the gentle sounds of running water nearby.

Follow the path that is in front of you. The sun is warm overhead and you can hear the chirping of birds and insects in the grasses. Walk along this path, putting one foot in front of the other. Feel the heat on your skin and the tickle of grasses along your skin as you step along the path. (Pause.)

Ahead of you on the path is a cabin. It is simple and modest, but well cared for. The door creaks open and Moving Robe Woman steps out and moves toward you. (Pause.)

Take a moment to speak with her and see what wisdom she can offer you in this moment about your own warrior nature. Find out what is most important for you to know right now for the path that you are walking. (Long pause.)

Moving Robe Woman holds out a gift for you to carry into the battles of your own life. You take it. Express your gratitude and speak any last questions that you are holding in your heart.

The time in this realm is limited. When you are ready, offer your gratitude to Moving Robe Woman and say any last things that need to be said. (Pause.)

Turn and find your way back to the path that brought you to her cabin. Place one foot in front of the other and follow the path that winds through the tall grasses on the rolling hills. As you walk, notice that your witch's eye is returning to its normal state. As it closes, you become more and more aware of your physical body. (Pause.)

Take a deep breath and notice the edges of your body, firm and in place. Take a moment to connect with the bottoms of your feet and the top of your head. As you breathe, notice your belly and the back of your neck. Use the palms of your hands to press against your eyes. Say your name out loud three times and slowly open your eyes. Take a look around the space that you are in.

Welcome back!

Write down anything important or interesting that came through for you during your visit. Take a moment to consider what information that was shared with you. What gift did Moving Robe Woman offer?

Return to visit Moving Robe Woman anytime you need help or advice for your own warrior path.

Being a Warrior with Moving Robe Woman

Moving Robe Woman is a true warrior. She shows us so many ways to find our own path toward living a warrior's life, which is also the path of the rebel. She fought for her people. She fought against tides of oppression and colonialism. These are not easy things to fight against.

And an important part of her story—a part that did not happen for many others involved in the battle—is that her life went on. There may have been other battles she had to fight after the Battle of Little Big Horn, but we don't know about those. What we do know is that she found herself living a peaceful life until old age.

There was a time for fighting and there was a time to live. It is for this reason that I find she is such an excellent ally when you need direction on your own warrior path.

The awareness of grief is such a big part of her story. We are lucky to have Moving Robe Woman's actual words about what she experienced. Most often, warrior tales are all about the throes of battle with very little acknowledgment of emotion or how the fighting impacted others.

We know Moving Robe Woman experienced grief, and she can also show us how to use grief as a tool. When life feels too hard or overwhelming, Moving Robe Woman can show us the way to move forward from a place of strength.

✦ ✦ ✦ Warrior Contemplation ✦ ✦ ✦

Where in your life can you connect with your grief as power like Moving Robe Woman? Are there things in your life that you will stand up and fight for no matter what? Are there places in your life where you need to stand up for yourself more?

Take a moment to look at the boundaries you have in your life. This includes boundaries with lovers, friends, coworkers, children, and even with yourself. Are there places where your boundaries need to be stronger? Are there places where you need to make some shifts and adjustments?

What are some steps you can take to firm up your boundaries?

Go and take one of these steps now.

CHAPTER 15

HARRIET TUBMAN

To say the education specifically focused on Black history in the United States is severely lacking would be an understatement. However, many of us have heard the name Harriet Tubman. Harriet, also known as Moses and General, was a conductor on the Underground Railroad for ten or eleven years. She helped hundreds of people escape enslavement and find their way north to have freedom and liberation. She was a devout Christian woman who repeatedly put her life on the line to help others escape slavery, as she successfully escaped on her own. A true warrior if there ever was one.

Harriet was born in 1822 in Maryland. Her birth name was Araminta Ross, and for most of her childhood, she was called Minty. Harriet's grandmother, who was from Ghana, had been kidnapped and brought to America on a slave ship. Harriet's mother was then born into slavery, as was Harriet. She was greatly influenced by her African lineage through her grandmother and mother. Although she had developed a deep and profound relationship with the Christian God, the magick and mysticism she practiced and believed in came from what she learned of her African roots.

As a child, Harriet Tubman had already experienced horrors no one ever should. At the age of fifteen, Harriet was intentionally struck in the head by a neighboring slave owner and suffered serious, potentially life threatening, injuries. She was not given proper medical care and came close to dying. Some believe it was this injury that caused her to hear voices and have visions and prophetic dreams.

In her late teens she was granted permission to hire herself out. This gave her the opportunity to work with her father, Ben Ross, on the docks and with timber loggers. It was during this time she learned the language and secret coding folks in those industries used. She also heard these workers talking about safe harbors for those escaping enslavement along the coast as well as places that were known to be dangerous.[28]

In 1844 Harriet married a freeman of color named John Tubman. He had earned his freedom by working off indentured servitude and was sponsored by a local church. There is little known about this relationship. Even though she had married a freeman, Harriet was still enslaved. She lived in constant fear of being sold south, which would take her away from her family and potentially put her in even harsher conditions. Plus, if the married couple had any children, those children would have been considered property of Harriet's slave owner.

Rumors started circulating that Harriet was likely to be sold, so she prayed and prayed and prayed that the man who owned her on paper would change his mind. However, the looming fear of being sent away was still present. Harriet felt that her prayers

---

28. Utu, *Conjuring Harriet "Mama Moses" Tubman*, 12.

weren't working, so she switched up her prayer and started praying for her owner's death. A week later, that man died from an unknown illness.

With the slave owner dead, circumstances did indeed take a turn, but instead of getting good news, things became a lot more complicated for Harriet. The odds were that she and her family would all be sold off, likely to different plantations. It was at this moment Harriet realized the time had come; she would not put up with this life any longer.

Stories say Harriet begged her husband to run north with her and her family, but John wouldn't go. He was a freeman, he had a thriving business, and he didn't want to live a life on the run.[29] So Harriet fled in the night, leaving on a journey that would take her ninety miles north to Pennsylvania, where slavery was illegal. This amount of travel could take up to three weeks on foot. She did it alone, leaving behind everyone she loved. She made it, and she never saw John Tubman again.

Once Harriet had her own freedom, she was committed to helping others find freedom as well.

She returned to Maryland to secretly collect her family and friends. Harriet made this run time and time again, creating a legendary name for herself. She was known to carry a pistol for protection and used the stars to guide her along the path. Stories started to spread about how Harriet had charms, mysticism, and magick. Harriet would pray and listen for the voice of God, then would follow the advice of the visions and voices that came to her. She seemed to be a cunning woman with a preternatural sense about things.

---

29. Utu, *Conjuring Harriet "Mama Moses" Tubman*, 14.

Harriet was just one conductor on the Underground Railroad. There were many others, and there were safe houses all along the United States where escaped enslaved people could safely hide out during their journey to freedom. Harriet was one of many doing the work of liberation, but she was one of the most successful. By the end of her nineteenth journey, she had a bounty of $40,000 on her head. In today's world, that would equate to $1.2 million.

In 1850 the United States Congress passed the Fugitive Slave Act, which levied serious penalties against anyone aiding or abetting escaped enslaved people. Even though the risks were enormous, Harriet kept returning to "slave states" to rescue others. Before the Fugitive Slave Act, escaped enslaved people just had to make it to a "free state," like New York, to be legally free. But after the Fugitive Slave Act, there were no safe states. Because of this, Harriet moved the final stop on her part of the Underground Railroad to St. Catharine's, Ontario. St. Catharine's was deep enough into Canada that it was very unlikely that bounty hunters would go that far north looking for escaped enslaved people.

Although she was unhappy with the United States government, when the Civil War broke out in 1861, Harriet left Canada to help the Union army. She enlisted as a nurse and used her skills with herbs and prayer to help injured soldiers. She was often described by wounded soldiers as having "the charm."

After the Emancipation Proclamation was issued in 1863, declaring all enslaved people free, Harriet had renewed vigor in helping the Union army. She led an assault in the Combahee ferry raid, which was a riverboat military operation that freed over 700 enslaved people. She was the first woman to lead an armed assault during the entire civil war.

Even after all she gave to the United States, it wasn't until thirty years later that Harriet finally received official military pension and commendation from the government.

Harriet lived in upstate New York. She remarried, a man named Nelson Davis. Near the end of her life, she was surrounded by as much of her family as she was able to recover. After the Civil War, she became heavily involved with the women's suffrage movement. She died from pneumonia in 1913.

Harriet left behind the legacy of a warrior woman. She saved hundreds—one could argue thousands—of lives and inspired hundreds of thousands more. Harriet Tubman is remembered as a brave and stalwart warrior that fought for equality.

OF EQUALITY AND CHARMS

Harriet walked her talk. Remember integrity? She not only saw injustice, she lived it. And when she said no more, she didn't just run and cover her own ass. She put herself in danger time and time again to help others. She extended a hand to help people find a better way.

Harriet didn't wait for "the powers that be" to fix the issue. She didn't wait for the government to fix the problem. She didn't wait for the slave owners to see the light of day and decide owning people was wrong. Instead, she saw her own power and decided, *Nope, I might not be able to change all of these bigger issues, but I can make the difference one life—one human—at a time.* She not only spoke her truth, she lived it.

Harriet was well known for her charm(s). She had a way about her that called folks to her. She also seemed to just have information and clarity about what was going on in a situation. And legends are not shy about making these abilities sound like magickal abilities.

Equality

I was raised in an interracial household. When I was a teenager, I dated a boy whose family was racist. (I didn't know that at the time; if I had known, I wouldn't have dated him.) I still clearly remember one awful dinner at his house with his family. His mother and her friend went on and on saying terrible, ugly, racist things. They knew exactly what they were doing; they knew who my family was. They laughed at how uncomfortable it made me.

I remember sitting at that dinner table with a lump in my throat, fighting back tears because they were being so cruel and rude. However, the worst part about the whole event was that I said nothing. I sat there choking on my anger, afraid to do or say anything.

I think back on that dinner a lot. I wish I could go back and give my younger self a boost of bravery. I wish I could go back and tell those bigoted old bitches where they could shove it. I've regretted not speaking up ever since. But that girl wasn't brave, she was afraid. It took many years of self-reflection, personal improvement work, and witchcraft to show her how to be brave.

And that's not the only time I was afraid to speak the truth or stand up for something clearly wrong. That's not the only example from my life where I let something slide. That's not the only moment I look back on with regret.

A witch, heretic, and warrior knows that looking back can give us information, but looking back doesn't change anything. The past is what it is and regret solves nothing. Rebels look forward. They look at what can be and they fight for that. It takes power to speak the truth and say the scary or hard thing. There's a famous quote from Maggie Kuhn that goes, "Speak your mind—even if your voice shakes."[30] That is the work of the warrior.

That young, scared girl is not present-day me. I am often the person in a group situation who says the hard or uncomfortable thing that everyone is thinking, but no one wants to say. I call out bad behavior or an abusive situation when it needs to be called out. Speaking out still scares me sometimes, but fear is not enough to stop me.

Fighting for what is right isn't easy, but it is worth it.

SPEAKING TRUTH

We all have times in our lives where we aren't being completely honest with others or with ourselves. We all allow bad behaviors to go on too long. We stay in situations where things aren't working because sometimes it is easier to keep pretending it's all okay.

Give yourself some space to sit down and meditate on your life and where you aren't being fully honest. What areas of your life aren't working? Where are you not being fully honest with yourself or with others? Now is the time to make changes in these places. Being honest with yourself is the first step.

After you've finished meditating, write down the places in your life that need an honesty upgrade. Then write a letter, either to yourself or the person who needs to hear the truth about what is going on. Write honestly, even if the things are hard to say. Give yourself as much time and space as it takes to make sure this letter feels complete.

If this letter is to yourself, read it over and make a vow to be honest with yourself going forward.

---

30. National Women's Hall of Fame, "Maggie Kuhn."

If this letter is for another person, read it over and see if you are feeling brave enough to pass it on to that person. Are you ready to share your fully honesty? Are you ready to speak your truth? If you feel ready, and if it is safe for you to do so, send the letter. If not, set it aside for two weeks and return to it. Reread the letter and see if you are ready now.

You might never feel ready to send that letter. It might be too hurtful for you or the recipient. You might need to really look at the situation and see if expressing your truth to that person is for the highest good of all. If you decide to never send that letter, burn it and release the ashes to the wind. Let it go.

Charms

Witchcraft is likely not something Harriet Tubman would have admitted to or participated in, but the stories we have of her show us that she was a mystic and a magickal practitioner. Yes, she was a devout Christian and had a beautiful relationship with her God, but she also clearly had spiritual experiences.

After going into prayer, Harriet knew where ambushes were waiting. She would get messages and know where to go and when to pick up supplies. She carried a gourd with her that was filled with herbs and plants, which she used in her prayers. And as a nurse in the army, she was skilled in healing. Sounds a lot like witchcraft to me.

The people that Harriet helped escape often described her as working with charms and having charms. In folk magick, a charm is a type of spell. It is an object that brings luck. It bestows better luck, health, and strength upon the owner of the charm. It's magick that anyone can access and anyone can use.

MAKE A CHARM BAG

Anyone can make a charm bag, and you can make one for virtually any reason. Just think of what you want to magnify or call into yourself and a charm can be created for it. In fact, take some time to do that now before moving forward. Would you like to make a charm bag for protection, love, success, money, or wisdom? Whatever it is that you want, be clear about it. Write it out.

It is best to perform the charm making on the night of a full moon. Depending on the current moon phase, you may be able to really take your time with the next step.

Once you know your charm bag's purpose, step one is to get a small square of fabric in a color that matches your goal. Ideally, your fabric will be about two to three inches on each side. Color alignments are as follows:

- **Blessing:** White
- **Communication:** Blue, white
- **Health:** Blue, yellow, white
- **Grounding:** Brown
- **Growth:** Yellow, green
- **Love:** Red, pink, lavender
- **Money:** Green, yellow, gold
- **Passion:** Red, gold
- **Power:** Orange, yellow, purple
- **Protection:** Black, silver
- **Road Opening:** Orange
- **Romance:** Pink, lavender
- **Success:** Yellow, purple, gold

The second step is to collect items, stones, herbs, trinkets, and curios that are in alignment with your goal. Your charm bag needs to be small enough to hide in your pocket or tuck into a bra; the bag will need to stay small and easily hidden. Keep that in mind as you collect your items.

In the following lists, I'll give you some jumping-off points, but take your time collecting the perfect items to add to your charm bag. Trust your instincts and use what you have on hand. Here are suggested stones:

- **Blessing:** Celestite, chalcedony, moldavite, sardonyx, sunstone, topaz
- **Communication:** Apatite, green calcite, howlite, kyanite, moss agate, quartz
- **Health:** Aqua aura quartz, fluorite, quartz, serpentine
- **Grounding:** Agate, black tourmaline, bloodstone, galena, hematite, smoky quartz
- **Growth:** Moldavite, rutilated quartz, tektite, unakite
- **Love:** Amethyst, celestite, garnet, larimar, rose quartz, sugilite
- **Money:** Carnelian, citrine, dendritic agate, diamond, hawk's eye, pyrite
- **Passion:** Chrysoprase, opal, quartz, red tourmaline
- **Power:** Chrysocolla, cinnabar, lapis lazuli, larimar, obsidian
- **Protection:** Black tourmaline, bloodstone, hematite, jet, obsidian, smoky quartz, tiger's eye
- **Road Opening:** Amethyst, obsidian, pietersite, red calcite, unakite

- **Romance:** Celestite, kunzite, rose quartz, quartz
- **Success:** Ametrine, bloodstone, charoite, Herkimer diamond, labradorite, malachite

And the following are some herbs you could add to your charm bag:

- **Blessing:** Dandelion, ginseng, sage, sandalwood, sunflower, tonka, violet
- **Communication:** Deer's tongue, jasmine, patchouli
- **Health:** Bay leaf, calamus, cedar, cinnamon, elder, eucalyptus, fennel, garlic, mint, mugwort, nettle, pine, rosemary, vervain, yerba santa
- **Grounding:** Basil, garlic, high john the conqueror, nettle
- **Growth:** Dandelion, flax, ginger, thyme
- **Love:** Balm of Gilead, basil, bleeding heart, bloodroot, cardamom, catnip, cinnamon, clove, damiana, elecampane, ginger, jasmine, lavender, myrtle, rose, vanilla, violet
- **Money:** Alfalfa, basil, bergamot, calamus, cedar, clove, dill, flax, galangal, ginger, honeysuckle, mint, moss, nutmeg, patchouli, sassafras, tonka
- **Passion:** Caraway, damiana, deer's tongue, dulse, galangal, hibiscus, patchouli, saffron, vanilla, violet, yohimbe
- **Power:** Carnation, devil's shoestring, ginger
- **Protection:** Agrimony, amaranth, angelica, barley, basil, bay leaf, blackberry, bloodroot, burdock, calamus, cedar, clove, dragon's blood, heather, hyssop, nettle, rosemary, sage
- **Road Opening:** Cedar, dragon's blood, sage

- **Romance:** Apple, bachelor's button, basil, catnip, cinnamon, damiana, jasmine, licorice, plumeria, rose, skullcap, thyme
- **Success:** Cinnamon, clove, ginger, high john the conqueror, lemon balm, rowan

You may also want to gather other bits for your charm bag, like coins, small bones, shells, seeds, or other little things.

Finally, on the night of the full moon, gather all your items together and place them in the center of your square of fabric. Don't overfill the square, as you will need to gather up the edges and tie it off to make a self-contained bundle. Wrap yarn or string around the gathered fabric and tie it tight—you don't want any of the contents of your charm bag to fall out.

Leave the bag overnight to charge with full moon energy. The next day, tuck the charm bag into your pocket, bra, purse, or bag. Don't let anyone else see it. Keep it hidden. If you lose it or if it breaks open, you will need to start from scratch and make a new one.

Keep this bag for as long as you need it. If you determine that your work with it is done or if it feels like it's stopped helping you, open up the bag and burn the contents.

WALKING WHILE PROTECTING

Harriet Tubman kept going. That is the mantra that has been held by folks who work with her: No matter what, you keep going. That is the message, that is the takeaway. The more I read about Harriet, the more I learn, the more I believe she was not afraid. And that's another theme we see with many of the women in this book. There is a sense of fearlessness.

I'm a big chicken. I have anxiety. I worry—a lot. So, I'm in no position to tell you not to be afraid. However, there comes a time when you must feel the fear and you do the thing anyway.

Harriet made her way to freedom. She could have found a job and carried on with her life, leaving the past behind her, but she didn't. She risked her life time and time again to help her family, friends, and total strangers find their way to freedom too. She helped them because it was the right thing to do.

Protection isn't easy work. There are no halfway measures in the protection game. It is an all-in or all-out situation. Harriet knew this, and she didn't play by half measures. One of the stories about Mama Moses recounts her telling the runaways there was no going back. Occasionally, someone running would get cold feet and think about returning. The devil you know, and all. But Harriet made it clear that they would either keep going or the journey for them would end right there, because she would shoot them.[31]

When you are doing the work and living the life of a warrior or rebel, you must keep your eye on the prize. You must protect what you are looking out for. There can be no other option.

ᔪᕚ Traveling to the Realm ᕚᔪ of Harriet Tubman

Sometimes you need an ally to push you to action. Harriet made it clear that under her protection, there was no turning back. When you need a push to keep going, it can require faith and trust that your allies know better than you do. Asking for Harriet's support in this way is just one of the things she can help with.

---

31. Utu, *Conjuring Harriet "Mama Moses" Tubman*, 19.

Supplies: An image of Harriet Tubman and two glasses of water.

Set Up: Set up a small altar with the image in the center of the space. Set one of the glasses of water next to the picture as an offering for her. The second is an offering for yourself.

Let yourself be as comfortable as possible. Sit or lie down and have a blanket or pillow handy in case you need them. Turn off any distractions and make sure you can be as undisturbed as possible.

Trance: Breathe deep. Take a moment to acknowledge that you are alive. Take a moment to acknowledge that you are safe. Take a moment to honor those things. And breathe. (Pause.)

Let your breath sing a song of love to your body. Let each breath engage your cells with love and light and wisdom. (Pause.)

Allow that feeling of warmth and wisdom to swirl around you. With each breath, invite that calm wisdom to envelop you more and more. Let each breath increase your level of relaxation. Allow each breath to take you deeper and deeper, shifting your awareness into a place of expansion and possibility. (Pause.)

See a warm, relaxing light gather at the bottom of your feet. Watch as this light swiftly and easily moves up your body. It calms and relaxes every part of you it touches. This light moves upward, leaving you relaxed and calm, warm, and safe. The light travels up your body; up, up, up. Moving from your toes to the top of your head. Leaving you fully relaxed and swimming in possibility. From this place of possibility, open your witch's eye.

With that third eye open, see before you a path. It is late at night, but the sky glows in star- and moonlight. The world is lit up with an iridescent hue. You begin to follow the path, one step and then another carrying you forward. (Pause.)

As you move along the path, you begin to hear the creaking of a rocking chair and the low hum of a woman's melodic voice. Those sounds call to your blood and bones and entice you to continue along the path.

You reach a lovely small and simple house set at the end of the path. Sitting on the porch in a rocking chair is Harriet Tubman. She invites you over. Take some time to speak to this warrior woman. Ask her the questions you hold in your heart and see what wisdom she has for you right now. See what areas of your life you may need to push forward in and not give up. (Long pause.)

Remembering that your time in this sacred place is limited, take another moment to speak of where you are not being in your truth, where you need a boost of bravery, or where you need advice on honoring your agreements. Sit and listen to Harriet's wisdom. (Long pause.)

For now, it is time to leave this place. If you haven't already, offer your gratitude for the wisdom that has been revealed. (Long pause.)

When you are ready, bow with reverence. Then turn and walk back down the path that brought you to this place. One foot in front of the other, step by step. Notice the glow of the stars and the moon lighting up the landscape. As you walk along the path, take a breath and let your witch's eye slowly close, returning back to normal.

Shift your awareness back to your body. Feel your body where you are sitting or lying down. Feel the weight of your bones and the weight of gravity. Take a deep breath and feel the firmness of your body as you fully return to yourself.

Tap the edges of your body. Place your hands on top of your head and say your name out loud three times. When you feel ready, slowly open your eyes and look around the room.

Welcome back!

Drink the entire glass of water, taking however long you need. Leave the image of Harriet Tubman and the offering glass out for her for as long as you feel called to do so. When you are ready, pour the offering water out in a sacred place. This could be into a plant, at a crossroads, or into a running body of water.

Being a Warrior with Harriet Tubman

Harriet Tubman shows us how to be warriors by teaching us the tools of passion, justice, and steadfastness. She. Kept. Going. One of the things about a warrior is that they know when to fight, when to run, and when to rest. There is a theme here as we look at all these powerful rebel women: They all knew how to listen to their gut.

This is the power of Harriet that we can all learn from. When we are fueled by our connection to doing what is right, when we hear the call of justice, when we know that we must keep on keeping on, that is the voice of Harriet and her power whispering to us. It is not about love or kindness or caring. It is about change. It is about fighting and doing what is right.

I know, I know. You are already saying, "But who determines what is right?"

Well, that question might seem pretty challenging, but here is a simple metric for you to determine if something is wrong:

- It is out of alignment with your personal integrity?
- Is it causing harm to others?
- Will this cause damage to the generations ahead?

If you have answered yes to any of these three questions, then you are not doing what is right.

True warriors, those with a rebel's heart, don't want to fight. They don't want to have to push back or be in the fray, but they do it because it must be done.

✦ ✦ ✦ Warrior Contemplation ✦ ✦ ✦

Where in your life can you see yourself fight for what is right like Harriet Tubman? Where in your life do you need an ally, or need to *be* an ally, like Harriet Tubman? Take some time to write a list of your allies, both human and nonhuman alike. Who can you depend on? Who can kick your butt when needed? Who can you turn to when you feel stuck, alone, broken, or lost?

Reach out to one of these allies and let them know what they mean to you.

If you look at this list and see lack, what can you do to change that right now? Call in the ally that you need.

CONCLUSION

Are you ready to claim the title of rebel? Are you ready to take on the world and fight against injustice? Are you ready to be the best you that you can possibly be? Now is the time, friends. Now is the time.

The growing interest in witchcraft gives me hope that more people want to take control of their lives. More people want to see real change in the world. We witches don't sit idly by and let terrible things happen, not in our own lives nor in the greater world around us. We witches have practiced our craft so we can make things happen. Let's not let those skills go to waste or be in vain.

Again, I truly believe that the more we know ourselves and do the good work of personal self-exploration, the better witches and magickal practitioners we will be. If you put in the time and energy to know thyself, your spells will go smoother, your workings will be easier, and you'll start manifesting like a badass. Self-exploration is such an important part of walking the path of the witch and the rebel.

This is the first step of living a rebel life. Do the inner work. Heal the inner landscape. And then go and kick some ass. We rebels and heretics know what needs to be done to change the world because we have already done that work for (and on) ourselves. Is it hard? Yes. It is worth it? Hell yes.

Bravery is the next step, which asks us to be vulnerable and authentic in all facets of our life. Then, if you're feeling brave enough, pick a rebellious inspiration. Perhaps one of the witches, heretics, or warriors from this book can help guide you?

Once you're ready, it's time to take on the world. Share your power with those around you. Shine like a beacon, calling other rebels into the fold. Make big waves and big changes so the world can shift in positive ways. You possess the power.

The time has come, rebels. The world needs you. The changes are happening now. Do you want to be part of the tide of revolution?

Let's ride, witches, let's ride ...

ACKNOWLEDGMENTS

I am blessed to know some amazing, witchy, heretical warrior women. First and foremost is my mom, Catherine. She's a badass and always has been. She then shared this trait with me and my sister. My sister, Jessica, is another badass woman I am lucky to know. Then there's my step-daughter Amy, who I think has been a warrior woman since birth. The fruit of my own loins, Trinity, is completely heretical and she expresses that in the gentlest of ways.

I also must call out some of my witchy kinfolk: Root, Amoret, Madrone, RoseMay Dance, Cypress Fae, Honeycomb Heart, Copper Persephone, Diana MelisaBee, Heidi, Ravyn, Suzanne, Gwydion, Todd, Willow, Jennifer, Seed, Urania, Ella, Tendrils, Sacred Chaos, and countless other Reclaiming witches that held me, taught me, and guided me along the path.

So much gratitude to my first coven sister, Keri, who has always been a heretical, witchy warrior. If not for her willingness to explore magick and witchery, who knows where I would have ended up.

Huge love to Daily Little. A powerhouse and constant inspiration. Every conversation we have leaves me feeling inspired and excited to grow and achieve my heart's desires.

Gratitude to Jennifer Untalan. Warrior woman and badass tattoo artist. She is a constant source of understanding and inspiration.

To the delightful and occasionally strict Gwion Raven, who helped me with editing and getting my messy thoughts into something coherent. Thanks love, you're the Swayzest.

Baba Yaga watched every word of this book as they flowed out of my fingers and onto a computer screen. She is the ultimate witch, heretic, and warrior woman. Hail Baba!

Heather Greene, thanks. Seriously, thank you so much. Quite the heretic herself!

Super grateful to all of the folks at Llewellyn whose unseen fingerprints are all over this project…

RECOMMENDED READING

There are lots of books that can ignite the rebellious nature in all of us. The following books will inspire you. They are a mix of fiction and nonfiction, spiritual and fun. Each one can help you to connect to something beyond yourself and add another spark to the calling you feel for change.

NONFICTION

Orishas, Goddesses, and Voodoo Queens: The Divine Feminine in the African Religious Traditions by Lilith Dorsey

A deep, devotional dive into powerful women of color in the forms of priestesses, leaders, and goddesses. It's a love note to the orishas and an introduction to working with them.

Women Who Run with the Wolves: Myths and Stories of the Wild Woman Archetype by Clarissa Pinkola Estés

A classic book of women's story, myth, and power. This book has been inspiring people to understand their wounds through folklore and myth for decades.

Wild Mercy: Living the Fierce and Tender Wisdom of the Women Mystics by Mirabai Starr

Saints, sages, goddesses, and wise women fill the pages of this book. It is an alternative to the masculine spiritual forms that overculture is so used to; it is an introduction to another way of being connected.

If Women Rose Rooted: A Life-Changing Journey to Authenticity and Belonging by Sharon Blackie

A call to a different way of being feminine. A story of connection to land and landscape. A mythopoetic dive into the modern woman and way of life.

Braiding Sweetgrass: Indigenous Wisdom, Scientific Knowledge, and the Teachings of Plants by Robin Wall Kimmerer

Want to read a book whose beauty will bring you to tears on every single page? This is the book for you. Written by an Indigenous woman, this book is about relationships with the land and the health of that relationship.

What Would Boudicca Do?: Everyday Problems Solved by History's Most Remarkable Women by E. Foley and B. Coates

A fun and silly book that comes with pages of women, historical and modern, doing awesome things. A source of inspiration for folks of all ages.

The Body Keeps the Score: Brain, Mind, and Body in the Healing of Trauma by Bessel van der Kolk

An exploration of how trauma literally impacts the physical body. This books explores how to deal with that trauma in a way that rewires the brain and brings health.

Emergent Strategy: Shaping Change, Changing Worlds by adrienne maree brown

How do we deal with all the problems in the world? This book tells us. It is a self-help book that looks at how we can help society and step boldly into the future that we want to be living in.

When God Was a Woman by Merlin Stone

The story of the goddess and how she went from ruling the world to disappearing. This book is an archeological dig into the past with new and interesting views.

Daring Greatly: How the Courage to be Vulnerable Transforms the Way We Live, Love, Parent, and Lead by Brené Brown

Need to do some personal work on shame, fear, or judgment? This book is for you. A book that helps you shake off the fears of other's projections and boldly step forward in your life.

The Big Leap: Conquer Your Hidden Fear and Take Life to the Next Level by Gay Hendricks

What's holding you back from your full potential? This book will help you figure that out and smash through it. Find your zone of greatness in the pages of this book.

World as Lover, World as Self: Courage for Global Justice and Ecological Renewal by Joanna Macy

In order to change the cultural landscape, you also have to be willing to change your inner landscape. The steps to doing that are held in the pages of this book.

The Spell of the Sensuous: Perception and Language in a More-Than-Human World by David Abram

A book that sings to the senses and humanity's relationship with the wild world. This book inspired feelings of beauty and a desire to commit to taking care of natural neighbors across the globe.

Fiction

Dreaming the Eagle by Manda Scott

A historical fiction telling of Boudicca's story, written by a woman who has been learning the ancient tradition of "dreaming." This book takes you right into the landscape of the Celts.

The Fifth Sacred Thing by Starhawk

The story of a Utopian land surrounded by the terrors of a post apocalyptic world. It is a story of the better world that is possible and what could happen if humanity doesn't make serious changes.

Fried Green Tomatoes at the Whistle Shop Cafe by Fannie Flagg

Friendship, love, and protection. This is a story of the deep love that two women have for each other and how that held them both through the ups and down of their lives.

BIBLIOGRAPHY

Alvarado, Denise. *The Magic of Marie Laveau: Embracing the Spiritual Legacy of the Voodoo Queen of New Orleans*. Newburyport, MA: Weiser Books, 2020.

Blake, Deborah. *The Witch's Broom: The Craft, Lore & Magick of Broomsticks*. Woodbury, MN: Llewellyn Publications, 2014.

Brown, Brené. *Daring Greatly: How the Courage to be Vulnerable Transforms the Way We Live, Love, Parent, and Lead*. Read by Brené Brown. New York: Penguin Random House Audio, 2012. Audible audio ed., 6 hr., 30 min.

Crowley, Aleister. *The Book of the Law*. San Francisco: Red Wheel, 2004.

Cunningham, Scott. *The Complete Book of Incense, Oils & Brews*. St. Paul, MN: Llewellyn Publications, 1994.

———. *Cunningham's Encyclopedia of Magical Herbs*. St. Paul, MN: Llewellyn Publications, 1994.

Dorsey, Lilith. *Orishas, Goddesses, and Voodoo Queens: The Divine Feminine in the African Religious Traditions*. Newburyport, MA: Weiser Books, 2020.

Estés, Clarissa Pinkola. *Women Who Run with the Wolves: Myths and Stories of the Wild Woman Archetype*. New York: Random House, 1995.

Fields, Nic. *Boudicca's Rebellion AD 60–61: The Britons Rise Up Against Rome*. Oxford: Osprey Publishing, 2011.

Hall, Judy. *The Crystal Bible: A Definitive Guide to Crystals*. Cincinnati, OH: F&W Publications, 2003.

Hardorff, Richard G., ed. *Lakota Recollections of the Custer Fight: New Sources of Indian-Military History*. Lincoln, NE: Bison Books, 1997.

Homer. *The Odyssey*. Translated by Robert Fagles. London: Penguin, 1997.

Ives, Eric. *The Life and Death of Anne Boleyn*. Oxford: Blackwell Publishing, 2020.

Kennedy, Ben D. "Joan of Arc Quote." *Joan of Arc* (blog). July 1, 2009. http://saint-joan-of-arc.blogspot.com/2009/07/joan-of-arc-quote.html.

Kenyon, Tom, and Judi Sion. *The Magdalen Manuscript: The Alchemies of Horus & the Sex Magic of Isis*. Orcas, WA: ORB Communications, 2002.

LeFae, Phoenix. *Hoodoo Shrines and Altars: Sacred Spaces in Conjure and Rootwork*. Forestville, CA: Missionary Independent Spiritual Church (MISC), 2015.

———. *Walking in Beauty: Using the Magick of the Pentacle to Bring Harmony to Your Life*. Woodbury, MN: Llewellyn Publications, 2020.

———. *What Is Remembered Lives: Developing Relationships with Deities, Ancestors & the Fae*. Woodbury, MN: Llewellyn Publications, 2019.

Long, Carolyn Morrow. *A New Orleans Voudou Priestess: The Legend and Reality of Marie Laveau*. Gainesville, FL: University Press of Florida, 2007.

Lotzof, Kerry. "Are We Really Made of Stardust?" Natural History Museum. Accessed April 23, 2021. https://www.nhm .ac.uk/discover/are-we-really-made-of-stardust.html.

Maid of Heaven Foundation. "Joan of Arc & Charles VII: First Meeting." Accessed September 16, 2021. http://www .maidofheaven.com/joanofarc_charlesvii_firstmeet.asp.

Malachi, Tau. *St. Mary Magdalene: The Gnostic Tradition of the Holy Bride*. Woodbury, MN: Llewellyn Publications, 2018.

Moore, Emma. "Women in Combat: Five-Year Status Update." Center for a New American Security, March 31, 2020. https:// www.cnas.org/publications/commentary/women-in-combat -five-year-status-update.

Moura, Ann. *Grimoire for the Green Witch: A Complete Book of Shadows*. Woodbury, MN: Llewellyn Publications, 2003.

National Women's Hall of Fame. "Maggie Kuhn." Accessed May 13, 2021. https://www.womenofthehall.org/inductee/maggie -kuhn/.

North, Wyatt. *Joan of Arc: A Life Inspired*. Boston: Wyatt North Publishing, 2010.

NZ Herald. "Kiwi Boy, 7, Invents Wolf Holiday and It Has Already Gone Viral." *NZ Herald*. October 3, 2018. https://www.nzherald.co.nz/lifestyle/kiwi-boy-7 -invents-wolf-holiday-and-it-has-already-gone-viral /LD2BRDZDN2OZOJF4NSOK5UU4VM/.

Samantha, Bridget. "The Skull and Bones of Mary Magdalene." *Atlas Obscura*. November 27, 2013. https://www.atlasobscura .com/articles/marys-house-in-provence.

Starbird, Margaret. *The Woman with the Alabaster Jar: Mary Magdalen and the Holy Grail*. Rochester, VT: Bear & Company, 1993.

Utu, Witchdoctor. *Conjuring Harriet "Mama Moses" Tubman and the Spirits of the Underground Railroad*. Newburyport, MA: Weiser Books, 2019.

Zakroff, Laura Tempest. *The Witch's Cauldron: The Craft, Lore & Magick of Ritual Vessels*. Woodbury, MN: Llewellyn Publications, 2017.

To Write to the Author

If you wish to contact the author or would like more information about this book, please write to the author in care of Llewellyn Worldwide Ltd. and we will forward your request. Both the author and publisher appreciate hearing from you and learning of your enjoyment of this book and how it has helped you. Llewellyn Worldwide Ltd. cannot guarantee that every letter written to the author can be answered, but all will be forwarded. Please write to:

Phoenix LeFae
℅ Llewellyn Worldwide
2143 Wooddale Drive
Woodbury, MN 55125-2989
Please enclose a self-addressed stamped envelope for reply,
or $1.00 to cover costs. If outside the U.S.A., enclose
an international postal reply coupon.

Many of Llewellyn's authors have websites with additional information and resources. For more information, please visit our website at http://www.llewellyn.com.